From Mean Streets

'There is a serious area of deprivation here, a cycle of poverty … which is leading people … down into the criminal milieu. … we have an army of alienated children just waiting for the call.'

President Mary McAlesse (then law lecturer) speaking, in 1982, of Southill, Limerick, in RTÉ's *Today Tonight* programme

'Undoubtedly Limerick's problems were accentuated by the housing policy that was pursued.'

Des O'Malley, founder of the Progressive Democrats and former Fianna Fáil TD

'It was kill on sight. If we got a phone call, we'd try to get one of them; if they got a phone call, they'd try to get one of us. It was blind madness. It was life or death. Them or us.'

Brian Collopy, RTÉ's *Prime Time*

'Where I teach, I meet students every day who have come from housing estates, where there would have been drive-by shootings the previous night. And they talk casually about going and bringing out their sawn-off shotguns. That sort of talk obviously makes teachers very nervous.'

A teacher at the Teachers' Union of Ireland congress, April 2006

'On the 10th of September 2006, my life completely changed, because on this date two of my eight children were badly burnt by a petrol bomb that was thrown into my car. Myself and my children did nothing wrong for this to happen, only I refused someone a lift to the courthouse. ... Doing this victim impact report and coming to the court lately means I have to start talking about what happened that day and it always makes me feel sick to talk about it ... While I was in Crumlin hospital, I watched Millie and Gavin going through intensive burns treatment every day.

'When they were coming off the sedation, they were in terrible pain, but I had to be there to support them along with the medical staff. Most of the time I had to leave the room, because I couldn't stand to watch them any more. ... They will be scarred physically for the rest of their lives and apart from the psychological effects it has had and will have on them.'

Sheila Murray in her victim impact statement

'The threat of the gangs to the State as it stands is nowhere near the level of threat that was there from the subversives back in the 60s and 70s. However, unless the problem is tackled it will become a problem of equal proportion, because it is inevitable that somebody is going to dominate the whole criminal scene in Ireland and the gangs in Ireland. When that happens, the person will be strong enough to organise all the various gangs in a way that will be impossible to combat. If we don't win the battle now against the gangs, we could very well find that we have a much worse problem in ten years' time, when not only will the battle be lost, but the war will be lost.'

Limerick State Solicitor Michael Murray

'They are killing people every single day, every time they sell drugs. What they are doing is wrong. ... You can't support the fact that these people sell drugs, you have to be clear and unequivocal about that.

'Drugs in Ireland have devastated whole areas and I will not be party to anybody who will give any succour to people who are selling drugs in my city. There can be no compromise with this and I am totally ... against it.'

John Gilligan, Mayor of Limerick

'Unscrupulous individuals at the high end of feud-related activity are targeting children and grooming them. These are vulnerable young people who believe this criminality gives them status as hard men.'

Superintendent Frank O'Brien, 2008

BARRY DUGGAN is Mid-Western correspondent with the *Irish Independent*. His proximity to events in Limerick has resulted in a keen insight into the intricate web of that city's criminal underworld.

MEAN STREETS

Limerick's Gangland

Barry Duggan

THE O'BRIEN PRESS
DUBLIN

First published 2009 by The O'Brien Press Ltd.,
12 Terenure Road East, Rathgar, Dublin 6, Ireland.
Tel: +353 1 4923333; Fax: +353 1 4922777
E-mail: books@obrien.ie
Website: www.obrien.ie

ISBN: 978-1-84717-144-3

A catalogue record for this title
is available from The British Library.

Typesetting, editing, layout and design: The O'Brien Press Ltd
Printed and bound in the UK by J F Print Ltd, Sparkford, Somerset.

Picture credits:
Front cover: Funeral of 'Fat Frankie' Ryan, September 2006
© Brendan Crowe.
Back cover: Emergency Response Unit,
courtesy of Press 22.
Picture sections 1 & 2: Press 22.
Map, p10: Courtesy of Limerick's Regeneration Agency

Contents

1 A Tale of Two Cities   PAGE 11

2 Concrete Jungles   20

3 The Top Dog & his Enforcer   28

4 A Feud Begins   41

5 Nightclub Bouncer Murdered   52

6 The Feud Erupts   77

7 The Murder Toll Escalates   98

8 Upping the Stakes   115

9 The Hitman Confesses   137

10 Moyross Arson Attack   154

11 Boy Shot & Uncle Murdered   188

12 High Street Ambush   207

13 Arms Plot Foiled   225

14 Innocent Men Die   234

15 Towards Regeneration   261

Acknowledgements

As my first venture into the world of published books, this could not have been written without the kind assistance of many people:

I am eternally grateful for the support of members of the gardaí who cannot be named and helped me immensely with their insight and research; they know who they are. A number of other people who live and work in Limerick and wish not to be named publicly for various reasons, I am extremely appreciative of their trust and input.

For all his assistance with the initial research and ongoing advice, my thanks to Eugene Hogan, and to *Limerick Leader* news editor Eugene Phelan who provided me with the most colourful apprenticeship after university.

In no particular order, I would also like to thank: Shane Doran, Abigail Reilly, Shane Hickey, Tony Purcell, John Hanna, Patrick Moroney and Anthony Galvin, and all working at the news desks of Independent Newspapers in Dublin, and my colleagues in Limerick for their help.

For their kind assistance and patience, Liam Burke and Marie McCallan, along with all the staff at Press 22, and photographer, Brendan Crowe.

I would like to thank my colleague, Ralph Riegel, for all his precious advice and assistance and for putting The O'Brien Press in contact with me. I would like to thank Michael O'Brien of The O'Brien Press for providing me with this opportunity. I am deeply appreciative of John Fitzgerald and Michael Murray for their assistance and co-operation with this. I would also like to thank Brendan Kenny and all the staff at Limerick's Regeneration Agencies for their help. Particular thanks are also due to Allan Crann BL for his invaluable legal advice.

I would also like to thank my long-suffering editor at The O'Brien Press, Susan Houlden, for the tireless work she did on this. While Susan is too kind to admit it, I am certain I left her with many late nights of endless work. Trying to untangle a labyrinth of information was only made possible and clearer due to Susan's experience and insight.

Finally, I would like to pay tribute to my family and particularly my sister Diane. When Diane volunteered to help me with this, she did not realise the workload that she was taking on board. She put a great deal of effort into this and it would not have been completed without her assistance and input.

Map of Limerick City, showing estates.

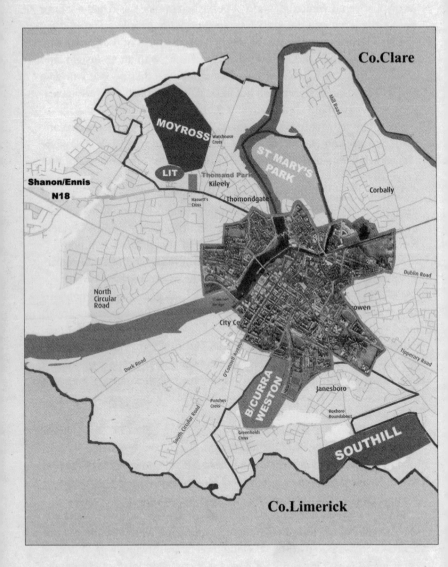

1

A Tale of Two Cities

On the night of Saturday, May 20, 2006, in the Millennium Stadium, Cardiff, the boys in red of the Munster rugby team defeated Biarritz to capture the prestigious Heineken Cup. It was BBC broadcaster Terry Wogan who summed up the depth of feeling in Limerick City that evening as he paused in front of a map of Ireland, during the Eurovision Song Contest, and fondly remembered the city of his birth with the quip, 'You won't find Limerick on that map. It's on a pink fluffy cloud at the moment.'

Tens of thousands of red-clad supporters from Limerick had journeyed from all corners of the globe to the 75,000-capacity stadium in the Welsh capital, to cheer their rugby heroes to victory. Thousands more watched the game on a specially erected big screen on Limerick City's O'Connell Street. When images of the packed main street were broadcast live to the Millennium Stadium, the venue erupted as supporters at the game united with those watching across the world and urged their team onwards to glory. Drinks flowed freely that night and for days afterwards. The following day, it poured rain at the team's homecoming parade, but nobody cared. This was one of Limerick's finest hours. For Limerick people sport is more than a pastime; it is a way of living, and the city has always remained faithful and devoted to its sporting heroes.

On that May weekend, the province's rugby team had reached the pinnacle of European rugby. If rugby is the gospel in Limerick City, then Thomond Park stadium on the northside of the River Shannon is regarded as hallowed turf and a revered place of worship for young and old alike. The enormous pride that Limerick people take in their home-place on sporting fields has often been remarked upon as a striking phenomenon. Stronger than simple allegiance and belonging, it is a feeling that somehow runs deeper, a true love of locality and parish through all tribulations. When it comes to local rivalry, its people take great satisfaction and pleasure in putting one over on their opponents. However, an attack from an outsider on one of their own, or, worse still, on Limerick in general, is regarded as a complete injustice and nothing binds Limerick people together more than an affront against the city, county or its people. This closeness, or loyalty, is a feeling that is all the more remarkable when set against the trauma and conflict endured by the city over the first decade of the new millennium. From the depths of pride to intense violence,

Limerick has known extremes, intimately well.

Less than a mile from Thomond Park lies the strife-ridden suburb of Moyross, where a few short months after the Cardiff success, an incident took place which sparked immense horror, outrage, anger and disgust. It is regarded as one the worst incidents ever to have taken place in the city and its events finally made the government and authorities sit up and take notice of the problems that were occurring in the socially deprived suburbs of Limerick.

On Sunday, September 10, 2006, Moyross already bore the scars of a weekend of mindless violence: a home had been attacked by arsonists, a man stabbed, gardaí assaulted, two squad cars vandalised, petrol bombs thrown and more than a dozen people arrested. The estates of Pineview Gardens and Delmege Park bore the brunt of the worst violence as roaming gangs of drunken and drugged teenagers and young men unleashed pent-up frustrations.

One of those arrested, and later convicted, was twenty-year-old Kenneth Sheehan of Pineview Gardens. He was sentenced to five months' imprisonment for assaulting Sergeant Eoin Gogarty with a Hennessy bottle.

Despite the violence and destruction of the night before, that Sunday afternoon the unsuspecting residents of Moyross still could not have foretold what was about to occur. Three youths had gathered outside Casey's shop in Delmege Park, Moyross. All were from the estates of Moyross. Sixteen-year-old Robert Sheehan (younger brother of Kenneth), from Pineview Gardens, wanted to go to the courthouse to see his brother who was up before the

judge for the previous night's violence. He was accompanied by a seventeen-year-old neighbour, Jonathan
O'Donoghue. Outside the small shop, was seventeen-year-
-old John Mitchell, a talented soccer player, who was
waiting for a game with local teenagers. O'Donoghue and
Sheehan had just been refused a lift into the city's courthouse by one of their neighbours, Sheila Murray. Sheila, a
mother of eight, was on her way with two of her children –
six-year-old, Philomena, or 'Millie', and four-year-old Gavin
– across the city to Garryowen to visit the children's father,
Niall McNamara. The mother had called into the home of a
friend at Pineview Gardens when she encountered the two
youths and refused them a lift.

Boiling with anger that she had not complied with their
request, O'Donoghue declared that he was going to burn
out Sheila's green Toyota Corolla. 'That would be the job
for her,' he exclaimed.

The three youths walked the short distance from the
shop to Pineview Gardens, where they agreed a plan that
would have far-reaching consequences and leave a nation
sickened and horrified. O'Donoghue and Mitchell climbed
into a back garden, while Sheehan walked over towards his
own house to act as lookout for any gardaí or patrol cars
approaching the street. It was his job to shout 'shades' to
alert his two accomplices should the gardaí arrive. Meanwhile, in the cul-de-sac of thirty-one houses, children
played on the street, while mothers prepared Sunday din-
ners. Nobody noticed the two youths clambering over the
fence into one of the back gardens. Litter and debris were

strewn across the garden and, in the rubbish, Mitchell and O'Donoghue found a petrol can, which had been hidden during the events of the violent weekend. The fuel container was not empty. Mitchell held a plastic Lucozade bottle in an upright position, while O'Donoghue siphoned petrol into it from the can. With the large bottle full, Mitchell stuffed magazine paper into the nozzle, to act as a fuse.

While the youths set about their makeshift petrol bomb, Sheila Murray emerged from the house. She thought it strange that the vehicle's rear window behind the driver's seat was wound down, and her possessions in the back of the vehicle disturbed. She recalled that O'Donoghue was at the car when she initially came to meet them, but thought no more of it. Gavin was first into the car and his mother placed him in the seat directly behind her driver's seat. Millie sat beside Gavin on the left-hand side of the back seat. Sheila then sat into the driver's seat, waiting for her friend to come out and join her on the journey across the city. She turned on the radio.

Hidden in the rear garden and standing on a mound of rubbish, Jonathan O'Donoghue threw the lit petrol bomb at the car. It sailed straight in the open back passenger window and exploded immediately. Sheila saw a flash behind her and her children, Gavin and Millie, became human fireballs. Petrol and flames covered the two as their clothing caught fire immediately and their skin began to melt at an intense rate. The car was engulfed in flames as the children's piercing screams penetrated the air. At this instant, the course of the lives of Gavin, Millie and Sheila

Murray, along with three teenagers, changed completely and, in one action, the innocence of childhood was cruelly taken from the brother and sister in the most horrible and unforgettable fashion. This incident would leave permanent scars on the children, and on the minds of Limerick people and the nation.

How had such a vibrant, modern, proud, sporting city become host to such an appalling and mindless act of violence?

Unfortunately for Limerick and, primarily, the citizens living in four specific areas, predominantly in city council housing, it took this incident for the authorities and government to finally recognise that a unique situation had developed in the Munster city.

It is estimated that Limerick City, including its immediate suburbs, has a population of just over 90,000 which makes it the republic's third biggest city. Limerick is one of the oldest urban settlements in Ireland and can boast a rich and proud history. The Latin motto for Limerick City is '*Urbs Antiqua Fuit Studiisque Asperrima Belli*' ('an ancient city well versed in the arts of war'). It has been quoted appropriately for a city beset by four sieges in the seventeenth century, and it still strikes commentators as pertinent when trouble erupts in the city.

Despite a city that has vastly changed over the previous two decades, it is the crime problem which continually drags Limerick into the spotlight. In the 1980s, Limerick gained the nickname 'Stab City'. This phrase has been heard across the world, leaving local politicians and civic leaders with the unenviable task of trying to deflect from the unwanted moniker. The exact origins of the phrase are disputed, but it was first heard in 1982. In October of that year, Thomas 'Ronnie' Coleman from Ballinacurra Weston was stabbed to death. No one was convicted of the murder. Two months later, brothers Thomas and Samuel 'Sammy' McCarthy died from stab wounds, following a fight in the Treaty Bar, Thomondgate. On Christmas Eve 1982, with the city still reeling from the death of the three local men, a Libyan student, walking in the city was stabbed with a screwdriver and died. A riot also broke out on the city's streets on the same night and the windows of more than a dozen businesses were smashed. Revulsion spread around the nation at the death of the foreign student, and one of the worst nicknames ever given to a city was born.

In more recent times, the phrase 'Limerick's feud' has surpassed the term 'Stab City'. The feud refers to incidents since the turn of the century when violence and gang warfare reached new crescendos. The decades before 2000 saw some episodic violence, but these events were separate from the frictions that dictated newspaper headlines at the dawn of the new millennium. A smattering of incidents, perhaps unremarkable by international criminal standards, would build up to become Ireland's most renowned gang war.

A primary factor in Limerick's crime scene is the extremely lucrative, but closely confined, illegal drugs market. Drugs had come to the fore in Limerick, and for the city's gangs, overseen by a few individuals, drugs quickly became big business.

Since 1990, drug hauls in the Limerick Garda Division have been on the rise. There were seventy-three recorded drugs seizures in 1990. Throughout the 1990s, the discovery of large quantities of drugs continued to increase steadily, and by the end of 1998, a record total of IR£1m worth of drugs for the year was seized by the Limerick drugs squad based in Henry Street Garda station. The same year, fifty prominent dealers from all areas of Limerick had been charged by gardaí, and 294 individuals were charged with drug-related offences.

At weekends, from the scenes in city pubs and clubs, it was evident that the confident Celtic Tiger cubs, who were out having a good time on the dance floors, were indulging in more than beer, spirits, music and each other's company. The advent of nineties' dance music had brought with it the associated drugs of ecstasy and speed, and, to a lesser extent, LSD. A single wrap of speed, or an ecstasy tablet, sold for about IR£10 and was easily purchased from dealers inside city pubs. Cannabis was, as always, widely accessible. One well known spot where dealers congregated was alongside a fast-food restaurant in the heart of the city. Here the dealers operated without fear of the authorities.

A 1998 study by the Mid-Western Health Board revealed shocking statistics with thirty per cent of post-primary teenagers in Limerick admitting they had tried drugs at least once. Entitled 'Teenage Smoking, Alcohol and Drug Use in the Mid-West Region', the report found that teenagers were more likely to experiment with narcotics if they were already regular drinkers and smokers, or if their friends used them.

By 1999 and the final few months of 2000, gardaí had made 332 drugs seizures, worth in excess of IR£3.3m. In one Garda operation in 1999, while officers from Mary Street Garda station searched for firearms, they found almost IR£200,000 worth of cannabis buried under firewood in an old military graveyard in King's Island. Officers investigating the find had their immediate suspicions as to who had hidden it. The individuals were from the city and had established themselves amongst some of the country's most serious criminal gangs.

Along with drugs, firearms became more accessible for criminals throughout the 1990s. Gun crime was becoming more prevalent in the city and, in 1999 alone, sixty unlicensed firearms were seized by gardaí in Limerick. Firearms were imported to the city on a regular basis with the supply of drugs and were often offered as sweeteners by those supplying them. Limerick's criminals had a ready access to a lethal array of firearms and shootings would soon replace the knife as the more preferred mode of attack.

However, there was a far more sinister criminal element about to come onto the streets and the estates of Limerick.

2

Concrete Jungles

An overview of the genesis of Limerick's hot spots is vital to an understanding of the city's criminal under belly. While serious crime has occurred in all areas of Limerick City and surrounding regions, the vast majority is generally confined to the four strongholds of the feuding gangs: St Mary's Park, Ballinacurra Weston, Southill and Moyross. All four city suburbs and estates were constructed by successive local governments in a bid to ease the ever-growing housing problem.

St Mary's Park

St Mary's Park is located on the northern end of King's Island and is the oldest suburb in Limerick. Before the construction of St Mary's Park, high unemployment and widespread poverty were clearly manifest with young and old living in squalor and disease-ridden tenements across the city. In 1932, the Housing (Financial and Miscellaneous Provisions) Act was introduced. This was a defining moment as it allowed local authorities to build housing for the working classes which the State would pay for. A scheme to build 480 houses at the northern end of historic King's Island was devised and completed in 1936. Each house cost £450 to build. Families who lived in Irishtown, Boherbuoy and the Abbey moved to the new suburb. It was the children and grandchildren of a small minority of these new residents who would later take a stranglehold on the city's underworld. Surrounded on three sides by water, the area became known as the 'Island Field'. St Mary's Park is made up of six streets which are all named after saints: Ita, Munchin, Oliver Plunkett, Senan, Columcille and Brendan. Athlunkard Street ringfences the entire estate. Once you pass by the grotto and the intersection at St Ita's Street and St Munchin's Street, there is only one way in and out of the estate, making it a safe haven for criminals and a place where gardaí have been routinely sent for countless investigations. It was here in St Mary's Park, under the shadow of King John's Castle and across the river from Limerick's historic Treaty Stone, that the city's first organised criminal gang would strive for control of Limerick's underworld. It was not long before antisocial behaviour gave way to drug-dealing and murder.

Ballinacurra Weston

The Ballinacurra Weston housing scheme was opened by Minister for Local Government Michael Keyes on

September 6, 1950, when the population of the city was estimated to be at 47,500. Constructed on either side of the Hyde Road towards the west of the city, Ballinacurra Weston on the city's southside was seen as another answer to the housing crisis for the city's ever-increasing number of young families. This new development was the product of slum-clearing and re-housing and by 1966 was home to up to 1,500 people. Even back in the mid 1960s, a study into this estate by Dr Liam Ryan, Professor of Sociology, NUI Maynooth, identified serious issues which were leading to wide-ranging social problems: 'The area is divided by a very wide main road running into the city. One observes imme-diately that the town-planners made ample provision for the movement of traffic, but unfortunately none at all for the movement of children. There are no playgrounds or playing-fields whatever, despite the fact that over half of the population of the area is under fifteen years of age. Pushed out of overcrowded homes by distracted mothers, the chil-dren wander around the streets in gangs. They have noth-ing to do, and children with no form of amusement automatically turn to mischief.

Southill

The infamous Southill estate was the next large-scale hous-ing estate constructed on the city's southside. Work began in the estate in the mid-1960s and it was finally made up of almost 1,200 houses. It is bordered by an industrial estate to the north and Rathbane public golf course to the south and consists of four estates: O'Malley Park, Keyes Park, Kincora

Park and John Carew Park. The main estate, O'Malley Park, named after former Education Minister and Fianna Fáil TD, Donogh O'Malley, was completed in the late 1960s and at one stage consisted of 600 houses, but in recent years, due to vandalism and destruction, the number has dwindled to 450.

There are two entrances to O'Malley Park at either end. Coming from the Roxboro entrance, an abandoned petrol station greets passers-by alongside the Olympic Arms pub. The estate – which often features in the news – sweeps around in a loop, and the vast expanse of rows of houses built during the last century can be seen from the foot of the hill. Some of the houses were built facing onto green areas with access for cars at the rear of homes. These back alley-ways and courts have become a haven for antisocial behaviour and illegal dumping. High security cameras have been erected in the area, but the majority of the CCTV cameras have been made redundant by joyriding youths smashing vehicles into junction boxes at the base of the poles and burning out the cars, making the cameras useless. Graffiti and signs of vandalism are rife across the area. Scores of homes have been completely burnt out and boarded up after gangs of roaming youths intimidated the elderly occupants into abandoning their properties. These same pensioners first moved to the estate with young families when O'Malley Park was constructed, but some of the younger generations are now driving them out of their home neighbourhoods. The Holy Family Church is located in the heart of the community and is also equipped with

CCTV footage and railed off from intruders.

In 1982 an RTÉ *Today Tonight* production shocked many viewers and opened the eyes of a watching national audience. The programme featured a presentation and discussion on social exclusion in Southill. According to the show, crime, education and poverty were becoming major concerns in Southill because of continuous government neglect. The future President or Ireland, Mary McAlesse (then lecturer with the Trinity College law department), a panellist on the show, likened Southill's problems to those endured by Catholic areas in Northern Ireland, following their abandonment by successive unionist governments. Speaking of Southill, she said: 'There is a serious area of deprivation here, a cycle of poverty … which is leading people, descending people, down into the criminal milieu. What I'm afraid of in an area like Southill … is that we have an army of alienated children just waiting for the call.'

Her warning has proved to become a reality years later. A well-meant 'surrender grant scheme' in the mid-1980s allowed corporation residents to purchase their homes and free up the housing list. The result was that those who could afford to left Southill. In their place, came people and families with poorer incomes, resulting in higher concentrations of poverty. By 1991, the proportion of lone-parent families in Southill (36 per cent) was almost twice the average for Limerick City. Despite the best efforts of community workers and Parish Priest, Fr Joe Young, antisocial behaviour and violence plagued the suburb throughout the 1990s. By 1999, gardaí had to escort postmen working in Southill, following a savage assault on one of their workers by a leader of a criminal gang. With the largest estate on the southside named after his uncle, founder of the Progressive Democrats and former Justice Minister Des O'Malley has described the Southill suburb as the worst example of social housing policy in Europe.

Moyross

The final large-scale construction of a single suburb undertaken to ease the corporation's housing list was Moyross on the northside. Work began in 1973 and eventually finished in 1987, leaving the area complete with twelve estates and close to 1,200 houses. Almost 4,000 people live in Moyross and it is estimated that half of the population are aged twenty-five or under. It is divided into a series of parks with a main road running though it, ending in the cul-de-sac of Pineview Gardens and Delmege Park.

Despite the fact that it had been broadly recognised at the time that mass building of concrete jungles would lead to poor socio-economic conditions, the planners of the 1970s ploughed ahead with the Moyross suburb. Objections were raised back then. Former politician Des O'Malley revealed, in 2007, that he had pleaded with city officials in Limerick not to build Moyross. He said that, back in the 1970s, the local authority was under pressure from the Department of Local Government to produce more houses and 'the only way they could do it was to build large number of houses on green field sites. … Undoubtedly Limerick's problems were accentuated by the housing policy that was pursued.' O'Malley believed the current regeneration programme which will see Moyross totally demolished was very costly, but inevitable.

By the early 1990s, with the Celtic Tiger about to boost the Irish economy, Moyross was already beginning to succumb to the stranglehold of the gangs, despite the fact that the estate was barely a generation old. In a Dáil debate in March 1992, the late Labour TD Jim Kemmy pleaded with the then Justice Minister, Pádraig Flynn, to allow twenty-four-hour policing in the northside estate. Such a proposal was greeted by the Fianna Fáil-led government as an over-reaction and an exaggeration of the problems encountered by the residents. Kemmy did not mince his words: 'This weighs heavily on me and I regard it as an indictment of myself, my fellow councillors and my city that we have not been able to tackle this matter.'

The proud Limerick man outlined that seventy houses were lying idle and were unfit for human living. He also told of single parents who were so frightened and intimidated in their own homes by teenage gangs that they had to flee the area. Less than twenty years after Moyross was completed, it was decided to demolish every single house in the maligned northside suburb and start from scratch.

By 2000, almost 40 per cent of the housing stock within the city boundary had been provided by the city council. Limerick in the twentieth century has been a story of local authorities hastily trying to find solutions to worsening socio-economic problems at a time when long-term vision and cohesive planning were simply not considered. The construction of mass estates to tackle the city's serious housing problem has been the bedrock for more serious and far-reaching problems throughout the latter half of the twentieth century and into the early decades of the new millennium. Problems such as gangland violence, antisocial behaviour and criminality have found a home in Limerick's concrete jungles.

3

The Top Dog
& his Enforcer

St Mary's Park was home to the Keane gang who were the dominant force in the Limerick underworld throughout the latter half of the 1990s. From this base, Christy Keane oversaw the outfit's operations which had established a vast, enterprising network across the city and country.

Christy was born into a large family in 1960 and grew up in the 'Island Field'. His mother, Theresa, is described as a dedicated family woman who attempted to instil a strong work ethic in her family. Along with his brothers, Christy ran a successful coal delivery business. Coal was delivered to homes across the city personally by Christy. The Keane brothers also traded in horses. Family members travelled to various horse fairs and sulky races around the country.

Sulky races involve a horse with a buggy, or 'sulky', attached and rider onboard competing against another 'sulky'. Thousands of euro are often wagered by onlookers and participants on a sulky race, which is also very popular amongst members of the travelling community. Had Christy stayed on the straight and narrow, it is believed he could have made a success of the coal business and horse trading. However, he became entangled in the darker affairs that were common across all of Limerick's under-resourced areas. Christy's criminal record dates back to 1978 when he was convicted of larceny in the juvenile court. He quickly became well known to the gardaí and had made regular appearances for burglary in the district court by the time his twenty-first birthday arrived. Through the horse trading and sulky races, Keane came into contact with Dublin-based criminals. It is believed he had close connections with the provisional IRA and dissident republicans. He was soon to become the main drugs importer and supplier in Limerick.

Anyone arriving into the 'Island Field' who was unknown to the gang was viewed with a great deal of suspicion and distrust. From the junction of St Ita's Street and St Munchin's Street, members of the Keane (often pronounced 'Kane' in Limerick City) gang could monitor and keep tabs on all who entered and left the estate. Anyone arriving or leaving must pass this point and teenagers were regularly deployed to monitor the streets.

Like all notorious outfits, the Keanes had a hardman, or chief enforcer, and Eddie Ryan fitted this bill perfectly. Eddie Ryan, like Christy Keane, had been born in 1960 and lived across from King's Island on Hogan Avenue in the northside estate of Kileely. In his early years, Eddie committed numerous burglaries and robberies, serving his criminal apprenticeship with Michael 'Mikey' Kelly, the 'hard man' of Southill.

Originally from Prospect, Mikey was born into a large family in the mid 1950s, before they moved to the new Southill suburb. Mikey became one of Limerick's best-known criminals. He graduated from robbing milkmen and grocery shops in his childhood years to become a young man with a huge physique which came in very handy as an accomplished street fighter. He progressed to assaulting gardaí and taking part in serious robberies and he became the focus of an investigation by the Criminal Assets Bureau (CAB) for tax and social welfare fraud. Mikey Kelly amassed more than thirty-five convictions and spent eleven years behind bars, before he was elected to Limerick City Council, topping the poll in the Ward 3 area in the 1999 local elections. He would later say of his partnership with Eddie Ryan that it broke up when Ryan turned to organised crime and became involved in the drugs trade.

In 1977 aged just seventeen, Eddie Ryan emerged from the Savoy Cinema around midnight and a short distance away became embroiled in a fight with another young man, Christy Jackson. Eddie stabbed Jackson to death. The following year he was convicted of Jackson's manslaughter and jailed for five years. His criminal list continued to grow and, in later years, he racked up further convictions, including breaking and entering and holding the proceeds of an armed robbery. He spent the majority of his early years in and out of prison.

While their Kileely and St Mary's Park homes were separated by the River Shannon, Ryan was never far from Christy Keane's side throughout the 1990s and became his trusted lieutenant. It was well known that Eddie was not afraid to inflict violence, or even death, on those who crossed his path. 'He was capable of anything. You would not know what move he would make next, particularly in his final years,' one source said. Eddie established a fearful reputation across the city as Keane's chief enforcer and was sent to carry out dirty work for the Keane mob. His harsh and punitive methods ensured prompt and efficient payments.

Crossing the Keanes was to prove disastrous for one particular family – the McCarthys. A sequence of events in the early 1990s illustrates how different families and individuals could come up against criminal gangs – and pay the ultimate price.

On February 1, 1993, twenty-nine-year-old Kathleen O'Shea was walking home through St Mary's Park with her husband and settled traveller, thirty-two-year-old Patrick 'Pa' Anthony McCarthy. On their way to their caravan at Canal Bank on Clare Street, Kathleen stumbled and fell into the path of a van driven by Daniel Treacy, a nephew of Christy Keane. The van struck and killed Kathleen, but the incident was treated as a complete accident by investigating gardaí. The Keane and Treacy families went so far as to pay for the funeral of Kathleen O'Shea. Following his wife's funeral, Pa, a chronic alcoholic, threatened the life of the van driver and demanded more money from the Keanes for his loss. It was a fatal mistake as nobody in Limerick puts the squeeze on the Keanes for compensation. Heartbroken and unable to cope with his anger and grief, Pa McCarthy, with his four children, left Limerick for Cork. He returned that Christmas to visit her grave and spend time with family members. Pa drank heavily throughout the holiday season. Three days after Christmas Day, he was travelling through St Mary's Park with his brothers when they encountered Christy Keane and his nephew, Owen Treacy.

Pa McCarthy began shouting and swearing and making threats, and a fight broke out, during which he was stabbed in the chest with a knife. His brothers rushed him to hospital, but he was pronounced dead a short time later. Keane and Treacy were arrested and questioned but later released and a file forwarded to the Director of Public Prosecutions, recommending that Keane be charged for McCarthy's murder. This, however, did not signal the end of the matter for the McCarthy family. Scores were not deemed to be settled.

While the rest of the country prepared to celebrate the New Year's Eve of 1993, the McCarthy family buried Pa and mourned his death in the caravan of his brother, Martin. Ten family members, including two young children, were packed into the small caravan at the Cooperage on Canal Bank and plenty of alcohol was consumed. At 10.30pm, two masked men – one of whom gardaí suspected was Eddie Ryan – appeared at the door of the caravan. One was armed with a handgun, the other with a shotgun.

In what must have been one of the most terrifying scenes imaginable, the pair opened fire indiscriminately at the occupants who had nowhere to take cover in the tiny home. Seven shots were fired, six from the handgun, one from the shotgun. By the time the screaming and wailing broke out from inside the caravan, thirty-five-year-old Michael McCarthy had been fatally hit in the neck by a bullet from the handgun, while his brother and sister, twenty-five-year-old Joe and twenty-two-year-old Nora, and his twenty-two-year-old cousin, Noreen, were also hit by the gunfire. The injured relatives were later released from hospital. Gardaí established an immediate motive, an attempt to wipe out all witnesses to the fatal stabbing of Pa McCarthy.

Speaking afterwards, Martin 'Manty' McCarthy was in no doubt that the assailants had targeted his caravan as the home stood out on its own. 'Manty' McCarthy told the *Irish Independent* immediately after the attack that he grabbed two knives from a drawer and chased the two men, almost catching one of them. Gardaí and authorities were dealing with a new phenomenon, a new breed of criminal, not afraid to strike terror and silence witnesses. Investigations on both murders moved quickly and Eddie Ryan, Christy and Kieran Keane were all arrested. On January 3, 1994, the same day as the removal of Michael McCarthy to Saint John's Cathedral, thirty-three-year-old Christy Keane from St Ita's Street, St Mary's Park was brought before Judge Michael Reilly at the local district court and was charged with the murder of Pa McCarthy on December 28 and remanded in custody. At Michael McCarthy's funeral mass, Canon Willie Fitzmaurice said the McCarthy family had returned to bury another family member and that many families in Limerick had experienced tragedy due to reoccurring violence. The homily offered by the priest would ring true for years to come as violent deeds continued to be inflicted from one family to the next with severe and deadly repercussions for following generations.

Gardaí questioned a number of people over Michael McCarthy's death, including one of the chief suspects, Eddie Ryan. Senior officers ruled out suspicions that the illegal handgun used had been sourced from subversive elements based in the Mid-West.

Christy Keane went to the High Court in Dublin on January 10, a week after he was charged with Pa McCarthy's murder, and successfully sought bail, despite the objections by Superintendent Liam Quinn that the accused man would attempt to interfere with witnesses if he was given his freedom. The presiding judge said there was no evidence that allowed him to conclude that Keane would interfere with witnesses. Keane was ordered to pay £1,000 bail along with an independent surety of £10,000 and had to sign on daily at Mary Street Garda station. When his trial began, Keane pleaded not guilty to the murder of Pa McCarthy. A number of witnesses testified against Keane, but their evidence was not accepted by the jury, and Keane was acquitted of the offence and walked out of court an innocent man.

Nobody was ever brought before the courts in connection with the murder of Michael McCarthy in the caravan, and the family of the two murdered brothers left Limerick shortly afterwards.

To be charged with the crime of murder was Christy's most serious brush with the law, but he would soon return to the focus of Limerick's most senior gardaí. As a result of the entire episode, the name of Christy Keane was known throughout the country and the mention of him struck fear into many. Keane was now on a pedestal and considered one of the country's top dogs among his criminal peers. From their investigations into the murder of the brothers, gardaí gained a greater knowledge of Christy Keane's empire. Keane set up a drug supply network across Munster, and Limerick was used as a gateway and distribution centre for the southern half of the country by his gang. Such were their earnings during the latter stages of the 1990s that Keane had to resort to hiding huge wads of cash in wheelie bins and safe houses across St Mary's Park. At this stage, Keane was married with a young son and daughter and his wealth was increasing on an annual basis from his thriving illegal enterprise. Gardaí also established in their investigations into the Keane mob that Eddie Ryan was working alongside drugs importer, Sean 'Cowboy' Hanley. Cowboy from Kileely had contacts with criminals across the city and had earned his nickname from dealing with horses and ponies.

Eddie Ryan's brother, John, was married to Christina McCarthy (no relation to the brothers murdered in 1993). Christina was originally from St Mary's Park and the couple moved into a house in the adjacent neighbourhood of Lee

Estate. Christina's two brothers, Samuel (also known as Sammy) and Thomas were stabbed to death, in December 1982, after a row broke out in the Treaty Bar in Thomondgate between them and Anthony Kelly from Southill. Anthony, the brother of Mikey Kelly who used to link-up with Eddie Ryan in their early escapades, was acquitted of the double murder.

In the early nineties, a car belonging to one of Christina McCarthy's sisters was vandalised, and one of Jack Collopy's sons was blamed. The Collopys, from St Mary's Park, were well known throughout the 'Island Field' and were close neighbours of the Keanes. Jack Collopy who lived in St Ita's Street, the central street down the heart of St Mary's Park, told the McCarthys that his children had nothing to do with the damage to the car, but tensions between the two families were stoked. The McCarthys came from Columcille Street which intersected with St Ita's Street. All those living in the 'Island Field' knew that trouble was brewing.

Jack Collopy was an ex-army man who had served overseas. When opportunity allowed, he enjoyed fishing and hunting. Shortly after the car vandalism, Jack Collopy's wife, Bernie, was sitting in the Moose Bar on Cathedral Place when she encountered one of the McCarthy brothers. A fight broke out in the pub and Bernie, the wounded mother, was taken to hospital, to receive stitches to a head injury. It was not the last time that the Moose Bar would be caught in the middle of Limerick's feuding factions.

Just over an hour after the pub fracas, a group of men appeared at the entrance to Jack Collopy's house in St

Mary's Park. Collopy later claimed seven men were outside his home, including John Ryan, Eddie's brother. One of the men was armed with a knife, while the others had a variety of weapons, including a spade. The lone man attempted to frighten the group off with an empty, licensed firearm which he used for hunting. It was no use; he was outnumbered and overpowered. The group wrestled the gun from him, and Collopy sustained a savage assault. He was stabbed in the stomach and shoulder by John Ryan and took a severe blow to the head from a spade before his assailants fled. The wounded man was brought to the Mid-Western Regional Hospital across the city in Dooradoyle. Such were the extent of his injuries that Jack Collopy was rushed to Cork University Hospital, where his life hung in the balance for weeks while he was on a life-support machine. The incident left him almost paralysed. Jack Collopy had to undergo intensive physiotherapy, to learn how to use his legs again. He identified and named his attackers to gardaí and a file was prepared for the DPP, but no charges or prosecution ever came about as a result of the vicious assault.

The situation in Limerick around the St Mary's Park/Kileely area was growing more precarious by the day. As close friends of the neighbouring Collopys, the Keanes, and Christy in particular, were left in an awkward position. The McCarthy in-laws of Christy's enforcer, Eddie Ryan, were totally embroiled in the localised feud against the Collopys. Before long, the Ryans were also drawn into the feud.

The Collopy/Ryan feud continued to escalate unabated. Christy Keane's daughter fought with a daughter of John Ryan's in a schoolyard row. This and other fights between school children are often referred to as the ignition point of Limerick's feud. Soon afterwards, a gunman opened fire outside the porch to the Collopy home as the family fled for cover inside. Jack Collopy named John Ryan as the gunman and said he was accompanied by his feared brother, Eddie. Attacks on property in St Mary's Park continued and the hatred between the families grew more intense.

John Ryan's brother-in-law, Patrick 'Pa' McCarthy (not related to the McCarthys murdered in 1993) returned to Limerick from Bristol for a family wedding in October 1997. At this stage, John Ryan was now embroiled in the intense personal feud with the Collopys and Pa was soon to experience it at first hand. Pa grew up in St Mary's Park, before moving across the Irish Sea in his late teens and starting a family in the UK. He caught the ferry home with his son and was in his sister's house in Thomondgate on Thursday afternoon, October 23, 1997. With his ten-year-old son, the pair called to Pa's mother's house in St Mary's Park for dinner that evening. Pa's brother, John McCarthy, arrived to collect him later from their mother's house. John had two nephews in his white Toyota Corolla car with him. Pa drove his brother's car away from their mother's house towards the entrance of St Mary's Park, but trouble was waiting.

As he drove along St Ita's Street, three masked men blocked their path and forced the car to stop. One of the men was armed with a shotgun. Pa hit the accelerator and attempted to escape from the area. The gunman opened fire, and glass from the rear window shattered onto the three children in the back seat as shotgun pellets flew over their heads. The occupants of the car escaped, but Pa suffered wounds to his back from the pellets. Along with his brother John, he identified those that ambushed them as three Collopy brothers, seventeen-year-olds, Philip and Vincent, and their twenty-four-year-old brother, Kieran. All were tried for the incident in the Circuit Criminal Court in 1999. The brothers denied the charges put before them and were acquitted by the twelve-person jury, following a short trial.

The hatred between the Ryans and Collopys was branching out to extended family members and associates. Throughout this time, allegations grew that Eddie Ryan was owed thousands of pounds by the Keanes, and vice-versa. Eddie found himself moving further away from his former partners, who were now making a stance and rowing in behind their neighbours, the Collopys, in the ongoing feud with the Ryans.

In a Limerick feud, the intense hatred of the opposing side is directly passed on to female members. It was no different here, and come the summer of 2000, teenage siblings from both sides engaged in arranged fights. In October, a daughter of John Ryan's fought and claimed victory over one of the Keane girls.

Within hours repercussions from the fight were felt as a number of shots were fired through the front window of John Ryan's home in the neighbouring Lee Estate. John

Ryan's isolated home was right alongside the Keane territory. Eddie Ryan called over to his brother's house
immediately after the gun attack, and the pair decided to
make their own investigations in the local neighbourhood
to find who had shot at the family home. However, as they
drove through St Mary's Park to pay a visit to Eddie's former
associates, gunshots were sprayed at the car and the windows were shattered. They both escaped with their lives,
but it was now clear that fist fights were to be replaced by
lethal firearms, bullets and bloodshed. The Ryans and the
Keanes were at war.

Despite the fact that there had been many personal dis-
putes between various families in Limerick since the
construction of the city's estates from the 1960s on, it was
the feud between the Keane/Collopy and Ryan families and
their extended relations, neighbours and associates which
gained the city a notorious reputation. Within a short space
of time, the local issues were replaced in the headlines by
far more disturbing affairs as bloodshed and violent attacks
brought reprisals and, in turn, more brutal aggression.

The Keane/Collopy and Ryan feud was about to turn
deadly and claim its first victim.

4

A Feud Begins

Eddie Ryan had by the latter half of 2000 cut all ties with his former boss, Christy Keane, who controlled the city's biggest criminal gang. The row which started out with his brother John Ryan's involvement in a local dispute with the neighbouring family, the Collopys, had escalated out of all control. The central crux of the dispute between Eddie Ryan and Christy Keane came down to power, drugs, money and who controlled it. The former enforcer of the Keane gang decided it was time to make his own mark and assert himself as one of the leading underworld bosses in the city. He no longer wanted to play the role as a contracted hardman but wanted to have his own slice of the action. To achieve this, he decided to eliminate the threat posed by Christy Keane.

After his spell in prison for stabbing Christy Jackson to

death, Eddie Ryan emerged determined to cash in on the lucrative drug trade. He teamed up with the Keanes and built up his reputation across Limerick as the feared enforcer, who took pleasure in inflicting pain. Married to Mary, they had three children, two boys and a girl. Their sons, Eddie junior and Kieran (known as 'Rashers') were soon both dragged into the family feud.

In Eddie Ryan's latter years, it became clear that not only did he sell drugs, but he also used them and regularly smoked cannabis. He maintained close links to renegade republicans and made no attempt to hide them. His relationship with the Kileely drug dealer Sean 'Cowboy' Hanley led to the trafficking and importation of drugs into the city.

As the undisputed crime boss in Limerick, Christy Keane now stood in Eddie Ryan's way. Christy's wife, Margaret (O'Halloran) was originally from the Garryowen area of the city, and the couple had two children, Liam and Natalie. The family grew up in St Mary's Park, before Christy acquired the plush, detached house at Singland Gardens. Liam Keane would later become highly involved in the feud and would spend many years in and out of jail. However it was Christy's ever-growing powerbase which led to a fall-out with his chief enforcer, Eddie Ryan.

On an afternoon in early November 2000, Christy Keane was parked along Shelbourne Road on the city's northside near Edmund Rice College, waiting to collect his sixteen-year-old son, Liam. Eddie Ryan knew that Keane would be there and lay in wait. When Ryan spotted Keane, he quickly strode up to him. Seeing his old associate, Keane wound down the driver's window to speak to the Kileely man but, within seconds, he realised that Ryan was not there for an informal chat between old allies.

As Ryan drew level with the parked driver, he took a 9mm automatic pistol from underneath his jacket and, in broad daylight, pointed it at Keane's head. Eddie squeezed the trigger, but the gun jammed. Keane didn't wait around and jammed his foot on the accelerator and sped off at high speed. One of the few witnesses to see the incident knew the two involved, but would not report it officially to the gardaí. He worked and lived in the city's northside and knew Ryan. If he agreed to co-operate with the gardaí, he knew that he would be severely punished by Ryan.

This failed shooting near the school has been recalled time and time again as the motivation behind the first life claimed in the bloody feud. The botched assassination attempt meant that Eddie Ryan's days were numbered. Fearing an immediate retribution from the St Mary's Park outfit, Ryan laid low for a number of days and stayed out of sight. He had taken to wearing a bulletproof vest at this stage and knew an attack upon him was imminent.

Christy Keane's younger brother, thirty-four-year old Kieran, soon learnt of the attempt on his brother's life and swore that revenge on Eddie Ryan would be swift and ruthless. Kieran was also well known across Limerick as one of the feared Keanes. With dark hair and a distinctive moustache, he was easily recognisable. He was also involved in the horse and coal trade business, but learned the criminal trade as right-hand man to Christy. Kieran Keane was married to Sophie Cross from the Dublin Road area of Limerick. The couple had two sons, Joseph and Kieran Junior, and lived on the Greenhills Road in Limerick.

Incensed that an attempt had been made on the life of his brother Christy, Kieran Keane set about to murder Eddie Ryan. The opportunity arose on the night of November 12, 2000.

A few days after the attempted hit on Christy Keane, Eddie Ryan had dared to go back into the city for the removal of his brother-in-law, Patrick Collins, at St John's Cathedral. Eddie refused to take heed of his brother John's advice to put on his bulletproof vest before he ventured out in public on that fateful night. After the short service, Eddie Ryan told family relations, including his wife, Mary, who was seven weeks pregnant, that he would see them later and went to the nearby Moose Bar on Cathedral Place shortly before 9pm. Across the city, Kieran Keane received a call on his mobile phone, informing him that the man who tried to murder his brother had just walked into the Moose Bar. Kieran now had the information he needed and his target within his sights. Quickly, Christy's younger brother set about making arrangements.

Kieran Keane was with twenty-year-old Philip Collopy in St Mary's Park. Like a great deal of residents in St Mary's Park and other estates in Limerick, Philip had an interest in horses, but was also an aspiring criminal, who would soon lead the Collopy gang, and become intertwined in the feud. Philip had already been acquitted of his involvement in the 1997 shooting incident at the Ryan in-laws in his home estate. In 1998 he earned his first conviction for handling stolen property. In May of 2000, Philip was convicted of criminal damage.

Less than twenty-four hours before Eddie Ryan was spotted going into the city bar, Keane and Collopys' associates had stolen a red Vauxhall Cavalier from the east Limerick village of Murroe. The car was an easy target as it was parked outside the sole pub in the quiet community.

That night also had life-altering consequences for another twenty-three-year-old man, Paul Coffey. At 9.30pm, Coffey, with addresses at Craeval Park, Moyross and Derryfada, Clonlara, County Clare, was driving his girlfriend and one of their children home when he was stopped by Collopy who said to Coffey, 'Come here. I want you to drive a car for me.' Coffey dropped his girlfriend and child home and returned to the arranged meeting point, where Kieran Keane lay in wait with ten men. Keane took them down to the family coal yard in St Mary's Park, and they picked up the stolen car. Keane and Collopy jumped into the car and told Coffey to drive the hot-wired vehicle the short distance across town to the Moose Bar, where an unsuspecting Eddie Ryan was drinking. The Moose Bar is located just yards from St John's Cathedral, across the road from the historic statue of Patrick Sarsfield. A large pub with a good trade, it was run by well-known Limerick publican, Pat Tobin.

When they arrived at the pub, Kieran Keane got out of the car and made a quick phone call to his informer. Upon completing the call, Keane said, 'Fuck it, [an associate of

Eddie Ryan] isn't there.' Kieran Keane got back into the car and instructed Coffey to move the car over in front of the busy pub. As they pulled up in front of the bar, Keane declared, 'If [Eddie Ryan's associate] is there, he's going to get it too.' Kieran Keane and Philip Collopy produced balaclavas and pulled them down over their faces, got out of the car and walked to the main entrance of the pub. They were armed with an automatic 9mm pistol and a magnum revolver.

The pub was packed on that Sunday night. Eddie Ryan was sitting at the bar with his back to the main door. Just after 9.50pm, one of Eddie's teenage sons, Kieran 'Rashers' Ryan, left his father and went to use the pub toilets. Within seconds, Kieran Keane and the other gunman burst in the main doors, identified their target straight away and unleashed a hail of bullets in the crowded pub.

Proprietor Pat Tobin later described the 'chaos and pandemonium' on his premises during the shooting and thought at first it was fireworks going off. 'I realised we were being shot at so I pressed the panic button,' the publican said. Fourteen rounds were fired at Eddie Ryan from close range, and one of Limerick's most feared criminals was hit eleven times.

Sixty-three-year-old Mary Reddan was socialising in the pub with her daughters, twenty-six-year-old Deirdre and thirty-eight-year-old Majella. Mary and Deirdre from Cregan Avenue, Kileely, were neighbours of Ryan and were sitting near the criminal. Both were struck by stray bullets. Other terrified customers and bar staff dived for protection as the gunmen fired openly, not caring who was in their line of fire.

Speaking after the attack to reporter Noel Smith of the *Irish Independent*, Majella said, 'I just could not believe what was happening. We were all absolutely numbed with fear – you would think it came straight out of the *High Chaparral*.'

In a statement made to gardaí afterwards, Paul Coffey stated, 'I knew they were firing at someone down low or on the ground.' The getaway driver got such a fright, when the lethal gunfire was sprayed in the pub, that he let the car cut out.

The gunmen ran from the pub and jumped back into the waiting car with Keane shouting, 'Drive, drive!' As the car sped away, the gunmen fired back indiscriminately at the pub, ensuring no one dared to try and give chase. Several bullets flew into the building through the pub window, but their trajectory was high and nobody was hit.

Within seconds, the attack was over. Eddie Ryan had slid from his stool onto the floor and rapidly began to lose consciousness. Seven bullets were lodged in his back, and his lungs and his spinal cord had been ripped apart. Near him, Mary and Deirdre Reddan were fighting for their lives. Frightened customers tried to assist them and stem the blood flow. Emergency services rushed to the bloody scene, but Ryan was pronounced dead upon arrival at the Mid-Western Regional Hospital. The mother and daughter had suffered gunshot wounds to their upper bodies and had to undergo lifesaving surgery. Gardaí said they were lucky to survive the attack. Eddie Ryan's son was also fortunate, in that he had been in the pub toilets throughout the attack on his father. A post-mortem examination was carried out on the Limerick man's body by Deputy State Pathologist Dr Marie Cassidy. It revealed signs of recent cannabis use by Eddie Ryan and a history of intravenous drug use.

Driving away from the scene at great speed through the city's streets, Coffey dropped the gunmen off at a housing estate in the Corbally area and promptly followed Kieran Keane's instructions to 'get rid' of the car, which was later found burnt out.

Gardaí immediately launched a major investigation into the murder with more than fifty detectives involved. The burnt-out getaway car was soon discovered, wrapped and preserved for examination. The scene around the Moose Bar remained sealed off from traffic for two nights as gardaí conducted a detailed technical examination and studied CCTV footage taken from the pub and the surrounding area. Bullet shells were discovered both inside and outside the pub.

Concerned that there would be an immediate retaliation from the Ryan side, extra patrols were mounted in the city. Parish Priest of St Munchin's, Canon Michael Liston, appealed to Ryan's allies in the Kileely neighbourhood not to enact revenge and said that further shootings would not solve anything. Detectives acknowledged that the attempted shooting of Christy Keane days beforehand was a crucial link in their investigation and appealed for witnesses to that incident to come forward. The gardaí were assisted by members of the National Bureau of Criminal Investigation. Investigators made a decisive move when seventy officers, including armed gardaí, raided houses across St Mary's Park in the first week of December. Six men and three women were arrested, including Kieran Keane, Philip Collopy and Paul Coffey.

They were questioned for an entire weekend and Paul Coffey made a statement to gardaí in Mayorstone Garda station. On December 10, Detective Sergeant Jim Ryan charged Coffey with Eddie Ryan's murder and the Limerick man was brought, under heavy security, to a special sitting of the local district court. The other eight individuals were released without charge.

It was almost two and a half years later before Coffey's trial was finally heard in Dublin Circuit Criminal Court in July 2003 after he decided to plead not guilty to Ryan's murder. Through his legal representative Coffey retracted the statement he made to gardaí about the night of the shooting. Prosecuting on behalf of the State, Tom O'Connell SC alleged that Coffey was part of a 'killing party', and that he aided and abetted the two gunmen by acting as the getaway driver. In the high profile trial, the prosecution's case was that Coffey was as guilty of murder as the two men who shot Eddie Ryan. At the court sitting, Coffey denied naming the two gunmen as Kieran Keane and Philip Collopy to gardaí.

Coffey's legal representatives admitted that their client did describe driving two men to the Moose Bar, without naming them. Despite his denials, the defendant's statement made to gardaí was read into evidence in court. Coffey said he did not know what was happening until he saw Kieran Keane and Philip Collopy pull balaclavas down over their faces just before they entered the Moose Bar and fired shots from inside the doorway. In another interview with gardaí, Coffey allegedly said of the murdered man, Eddie Ryan, 'He's like what the General was in Dublin. If whoever shot Eddie is found, he will get the same.'

On July 30, 2003, following hours of legal argument, the trial ended dramatically when Coffey pleaded guilty to Eddie Ryan's manslaughter. Eddie's widow, Mary, was in court to hear the defendant admit his role. Speaking outside the court, Mrs Ryan said she hoped those who were involved in the killing and had not been prosecuted would be brought to justice. Coffey, who had suffered learning disabilities at school, had previous convictions for weapons and violent offences, was a known drug addict and suffered from depression. He also claimed in court that he had been the victim of sexual abuse. On November 7, 2003, he was sentenced to fifteen years' imprisonment by Mr Justice Henry Abbott for the manslaughter charge, with seven years suspended, as he was described as the 'fall guy' and was 'easily led'. 'He was not the main player,' Mr Justice Henry Abbott said, in this 'heinous' crime. He said the killing of the father-of-three was a 'quantum leap' in the Limerick feud.

Coffey apologised to the Ryan family for his role in the killing and insisted he would not have appeared in court had he known what was planned that night. Smartly dressed in a suit, Coffey gave waiting photographers two-fingered salutes while being led from the building to the waiting prison escort. By the time Coffey had pleaded guilty to the manslaughter offence, the feud had spiralled out of control and the city's deprived estates had become out-and-out battlefields, where the warring opponents carried out their vicious attacks on each other. Detective Sergeant Jim Ryan told the court that 'every kind of criminal activity imaginable' had occurred since Eddie Ryan's killing.

The business of drug dealing and criminal activity continued in Limerick before the high profile case. Drugs seizures in the Mid-West region in 2001 came to €3m and €1.5m the following year. By the time Paul Coffey had spent his first night in his prison cell after receiving his sentence, over 100 incidents, including numerous shootings, petrol-bomb attacks, bloody assaults and three gangland assassinations had left the city shaken, with its reputation sullied and disgraced. The two gunmen, Kieran Keane and Philip Collopy, who shot Eddie Ryan dead in the Moose Bar, were never charged with his murder.

5

Nightclub Bouncer Murdered

The murder of Eddie Ryan was a watershed moment in the history of Limerick crime. It cast a long and dark shadow over Limerick. The gunshots that tore through Ryan sparked a series of reprisal attacks in St Mary's Park on the Keanes and, in turn, on the Ryan family and their properties in Lee Estate and Kileely. Violence inflicted by one side brought about an instant and sometimes stronger response from the other side.

On St Patrick's Day, 2001, a car jack was thrown through the sitting-room window of John Ryan's home in Lee Estate, Island Road. Three days later a more sinister attack took place. The Ryan family, including five children, were in their beds when gunshots came flying through two bedroom windows at 3am. The home was riddled with bullet holes, but the seven occupants escaped unharmed. John Ryan's wife, Christina, said her family was terrified and recalled hearing her five children scream from their beds as the shots flew into their home.

The attacks on John Ryan's home became increasingly worse. Their house was cut off from the Ryan Kileely and Ballynanty stronghold, and they were living very near to the Ryans' enemies in St Mary's Park. On May 17, fifteen gunshots were fired at the house, while the family slept inside, but miraculously no one was injured. Another gun attack on the home occurred on July 13 at 12.45am, when four shots were fired at the building. In the year following the death of his brother, John Ryan claimed his home was shot at and petrol-bombed on thirty separate occasions. His house became known as 'the Alamo' for the number of times it sustained attacks. Eventually, the family moved to temporary accommodation in Moyross. John Ryan claimed, in an interview with Eugene Hogan of the *Irish Independent* in 2003, that the feud had started when a family member beat up two daughters of the Keane family in the one day. He admitted his brother Eddie 'got involved then and tried to take revenge, but the gun jammed and days later Eddie was killed at a funeral. It happened within the space of a few days. It just blew up.' Ryan said the families had been friendly up until that point.

As the attacks in and around St Mary's Park and Lee Estate continued throughout 2001, armed Garda patrols were deployed to King's Island to prevent further bloodshed.

Garda checkpoints in the area became commonplace and all vehicles entering and leaving the estate were monitored by officers in a bid to prevent the freedom of movement previously enjoyed by the hoods in the estate.

Members of the extended Keane family also came under attack throughout the twelve months after the Moose Bar shooting, as the attitude of an eye for an eye and a tooth for a tooth prevailed between the feuding families.

On the evening of May 17, 2001, Philip Treacy was relaxing in his home at Clonlara, County Clare. Philip's wife, Pauline, was Christy Keane's sister. They were the parents of Owen Treacy who was often seen in the company of his criminal uncles, Christy and Kieran. Philip was lying down on a couch waiting for the 6pm news to come on when two petrol bombs came crashing through the sitting-room window. Pauline, two daughters, and a son along with a friend were also in the house. One of the petrol canisters hit the father's left arm and ignited. Philip jumped up and saw a man getting into a car, before it sped off. 'The place was blazing,' he said. 'I roared at one of the girls to call the gardaí. My wife came in screaming, the young fellow with my son was roaring, as was my son.'

Treacy, who worked as a baker and had not been involved in any trouble beforehand, raced to get a garden hose. He almost suffocated while he attempted to put out the inferno. There was extensive damage to the home from the flames and smoke, and the repair work was estimated to be up to €15,000. The arson attack had a traumatic effect on Philip and Pauline.

Gardaí moved quickly in their investigations of the petrol bombing. Within nine days, two young men and a teenager were brought before a special sitting of the local district court and charged in connection with the fire-bomb attack. Twenty-three year old Noel Price of Kileely Road, Bally-nanty, eighteen-year-old Michael Stanners of Delmege Park, Moyross along with sixteen-year-old Keith O'Dwyer from Moylish Crescent were all charged on May 26.

Two years later, Noel Price and Michael Stanners, deny-ing the charges, were jailed for twelve years for their roles in the attack. Judge Carroll Moran heard that the two men had previous convictions and came from deprived back-grounds.

Noel Price's father, Philip Price, left home when Noel was just thirteen years old. Noel Price was an unemployed father-of-one who had more than ten previous convictions, dating back to 1995. These included an arson attack on the car of an off-duty Garda, assaulting a Garda, possession of a firearm, and drugs offences.

Michael Stanners, who donned a balaclava before throw-ing the petrol bomb at the house, had previous convictions, including car theft. Detective Sergeant Jim Ryan said Philip Treacy was not involved in the feud and was considered to be a soft target as he lived in an isolated area.

Meanwhile, Keith O'Dwyer left the country following the attack and travelled to Lanzarote. He was eventually jailed in June 2006 for three years. Judge Carroll Moran was pre-siding over the case and was told that the accused was influenced by Price and Stanners and had not been involved in the planning of the attack.

Gardaí, who were now trying to contain the growing feud, had a massive break against drug dealing in Limerick on August 21, 2001, when they captured the city's most feared gang boss red-handed with €240,000 of cannabis. Christy Keane, who had survived Eddie Ryan's assassination attempt nine months previously, was walking through his home turf at St Mary's Park when he was spotted by Detectives Ronan McDonagh, Brian Sugrue and Eamon Curley who were on patrol in the estate. The well-known Limerick man was slouched over and carrying a large Bord na Mona bag across his back at St Munchin's Street and immediately began running when he spotted the unmarked patrol car. Detective McDonagh was right on his heels, however, and caught Keane as he attempted to drop the bag, which was found to contain four tightly wrapped cannabis packages. He was brought to Henry Street Garda station and word soon spread that one of the country's most feared criminals was caught so easily in his home estate. The quantity of drugs recovered – 19 kg – would have been capable of making approximately 190,000 joints and a substantial amount of money for its dealers.

In May 2002 Keane was tried and pleaded not guilty to the charges of possession of the drugs for sale or supply. The two-day trial at Limerick Circuit Court was hindered by allegations that associates of the defendant were attempting to influence the jury of six men and six women. Shortly after the hearing began, the judge heard Garda evidence while the jury were absent from the courtroom that the driver of the bus assigned to transport the jury to their lunch was approached by a man described as an associate of Keane. An alternative driver and bus had to be brought to the court house. On the same day, Judge Sean O'Leary ordered a person out of the court for acting in an intimidatory manner towards the jury.

Christy Keane, now aged forty-one, gave his address as Singland Gardens, Ballysimon, Limerick, and claimed to have been incorrectly identified by the officers from Henry Street Garda station and said he was carrying a bridle and rope for a horse when he was confronted by gardaí. In another twist, an inmate of Limerick Prison insisted it was he and not Keane who had been carrying the coal bag when the detectives arrived in the area.

The twenty-seven-year-old inmate, who was awaiting sentence for another criminal matter, told the stunned court that he was carrying the sack of hash. The prisoner, who was unable to read or write, said he asked another prisoner to write a letter on his behalf to a solicitor, admitting that he was responsible for the offence and not Keane. The letter was faxed from the prison seven weeks after Keane was remanded in custody to the same jail. The prisoner who had undergone a methadone maintenance programme for his drug habit denied that Keane had instructed him to write the letter.

Supt Gerry Mahon of Roxboro Garda station told the packed court that Keane was not a drugs courier, but a gang leader who had no known means of income and was living in a private house. On May 31, 2002, the father-of-two was found guilty by the jury on two charges of possession, and possession with intent to supply and was sentenced to ten years' imprisonment by Judge O'Leary. The judge said, 'I am satisfied and I accept that Christopher Keane is a substantial operator on the drugs scene ... on the upper end of the supply chain.'

After passing sentence, Judge O'Leary referred to the court atmosphere during the trial, which he described as hostile to the jury. The judge said he was not suggesting Keane was responsible, but he did not want it to happen again. The verdict was a massive success for the gardaí and the prosecutors as one of the biggest drug lords operating in the State had been put away for a lengthy period.

However, new challenges presented themselves to the authorities at every turn and another contentious issue arose in the final months of 2001. The problem for gardaí attempting to prosecute serious criminals in Limerick had gone well beyond the Keane/Ryan dynamic. Plenty of other factions were set on causing trouble also.

At this stage up to ten cases involving serious offences in the city had collapsed due to a peace pact between south-side feuding families. Self-reformed Limerick City criminal, Mikey Kelly, who topped the polls to become a local Alder-man in 1999, had brokered a peace pact between a large family from the outskirts of Southill, and another southside gang. Gardaí believed that, as a result of this brokered peace pact and similar other agreements, witnesses to serious crimes withdrew and changed their statements.

Following the collapse of a number of serious assault

trials, Judge Harvey Kenny ordered an investigation into alleged interference with witnesses. An outside Garda unit, drawn from the Cork division, was drafted in to carry out the investigation in 2001 and interviewed up to 100 people, including city-based gardaí, suspects and even a number of journalists.

Alderman Mikey Kelly defended his brokered peace pact and said that he was 'standing over' the withdrawal of allegations by witnesses, stating that without this the southside feuding would have continued. Kelly denied that justice had been interfered with. Ultimately, prosecuting anyone who may have perverted the course of justice or interfered with witnesses proved beyond the authorities after the Director of Public Prosecution decided there was insufficient evidence to bring anyone to court.

Meanwhile, the Ryan/Keane feud was festering and continuing to intensify. With Christy Keane locked up awaiting his trial and subsequent conviction for drug-dealing, younger brother Kieran Keane had taken over control of the Keane gang in 2002. His short list of offences was mostly of a minor nature, but his reputation stretched far and wide as a sinister and unforgiving drugs-lord. Kieran had no conviction for serious drugs offences and, like so many at the highest levels of organised crime, he managed to elude the clutches of the law for years while underlings and foot soldiers took the rap.

In early 2002, he attacked the Ryan brothers' mother, Mary, outside the local district court. Eddie Ryan's widow was head-butted by Kieran Keane, who callously informed her, 'I got your husband, now I am going to get you.' This was the only offence Kieran Keane was convicted of after the murder of Eddie Ryan. At this stage, Kieran had become the focus of an intense investigation by the Criminal Assets Bureau which was examining the sources of all of his wealth.

The feud was also passed onto the next generation. On March 5, 2002, seventeen-year-old Liam Keane – the son of Christy Keane – was stabbed in the back while walking in the city centre. Liam provided a statement to gardaí, identifying the son of murdered Eddie Ryan, Kieran 'Rashers' Ryan, as his assailant. However, he failed to follow on from his statement and did not identify Kieran 'Rashers' Ryan as his assailant when the case came before court.

Born on August 12, 1984, Liam Keane grew up in St Mary's Park, but left school after completing his junior cert. Liam earned his first conviction in January 2002 when he was sentenced to three months' imprisonment for a firearms offence.

With the Ryan/Keane feud intensifying, it was only a matter of time before further relatives and friends of those directly involved were dragged into the dispute. Gardaí had suspected that subversive elements had become entangled in the feud and were supplying both sides with a new array of deadly weapons. By 2002, Garda intelligence had received strong indications that armoury such as the Kalashnikov AK47 – a weapon capable of penetrating walls which had been used in conflicts across the world in Africa, Asia and the Middle-East – was being sold by the paramilitaries to the city's criminal gangs. Whereas two decades previously, the knife and other crude instruments were the weapon of choice, Limerick gangs had become much more sophisticated and much more deadly. The reason for this was quite apparent – it boiled down to a simple need for survival in a city where family feuds were far more deadly than anywhere else in the country.

Since the murder of Eddie Ryan, the feud had not resulted in any further violent deaths.

Luck had played a big role in the death toll not being added to, but much more significant has been the excellent work of gardaí in undercover operations. They had targeted leading gang members and succeeded in getting convictions and lengthy sentences against major players for drug offences and assaults. Unfortunately for Limerick, such was the gangs' readiness to use their new weapons that the feud could re-ignite at any second.

Further proof of just how far Limerick's gangs were prepared to go to eliminate the opposition was offered in the summer of 2002.

The incident displayed how intense the Limerick feud had become and how its main protagonists cared little for innocent parties who may be caught in the crossfire.

On August 23, 2002, 'Fat John' McCarthy, a nephew of the murdered Eddie Ryan, answered a knock at his front door in Cliona Park, Moyross, at 10.30pm. Three local teenage boys were outside the house and McCarthy, a father-of-five, went to talk to them as they sat on a garden bench. McCarthy had become extremely cautious since his uncle's murder and was very wary of any unknown vehicles entering the neighbourhood. Around 10.30pm on that Friday night, a white car, which had been stolen in the Killaloe area three days previously, came driving into the avenue. It slowed down at first, but immediately began to speed up once Fat John and the family home were within sight. Inside the car were nineteen-year-old cousins, Ross Cantillon from St Ita's Street, St Mary's Park, and Roy Woodland, Canon Breen Park, Thomondgate. The pair was armed with a loaded Kalashnikov assault rifle.

Cantillon was driving the car, while Woodland was the designated gunman and was cocking the rifle. Despite their youth, both were well known on Limerick's criminal scene and had been victims of brutal attacks in connection with the feud, which had resulted in devastating consequences. Woodland's leg was amputated, after he was shot twice in December 2001 on the Ennis Road. He was stabbed in the head in a separate incident. Cantillon sustained two perforated lungs in a stabbing incident and he too had been shot in the leg. Their family homes had also been attacked and windows had been shot through.

Instantly suspicious at the unidentified car entering the estate, Fat John McCarthy saw a gun barrel emerge from the front passenger window. He roared at everyone to get down as gunfire exploded in the direction of the family home. Eleven rounds were sprayed from the AK-47 with one pull of the trigger, and shots flew through the front door and a parked car. Fat John McCarthy's nine-year-old son, David, was walking down the stairs at the time of the shooting and one of the bullets missed him by inches and blew a picture off the wall beside him. It was believed by gardaí that this was possibly the first time in the history of the State where this type of assault rifle was used in a feud between families.

Driving on one flat wheel, Cantillon and Woodland abandoned the car at the nearby Meelick Tavern, at 10.45pm, before setting it alight. They were spotted leaving the vehicle by a customer and were arrested the following day and subsequently made a number of statements to gardaí during interviews. The following Monday at a special sitting of Limerick District Court before Judge Timothy Lucey, both young men were denied a bail application. The AK-47 was discovered hidden in a hedge and the finger-prints of the two culprits were found on the stolen vehicle. Part of the gun had been sawn off and the serial number was erased. Twelve live rounds of ammunition and shells were also recovered from the scene of the attack.

At the subsequent trial in Limerick Circuit Criminal Court, Fat John McCarthy, giving evidence, explained, 'I was expecting this to happen two years before it happened. I know that people are out to get me since they killed my uncle, Eddie Ryan, in the Moose Bar two years ago.'

The two accused initially pleaded not guilty to their roles in the shooting, but changed their pleas during the course of the trial. They told how they had rented the assault rifle for the sum of €400. Cantillon told gardaí he could not reveal where he sourced the gun as he would be killed if he did. They both maintained they did not carry out the gun attack to kill anyone, but to scare their targets with warning shots. Both men claimed that they had been shot and stabbed by members of the McCarthy family in feud-provoked incidents in the past. The court heard they were acting on the directions of a leading member of one of the feuding factions. On June 19, 2003, after almost a year in custody, the two cousins were each sentenced to twelve years' imprisonment, with the last five years suspended, for the drive-by shooting. When passing sentence, Judge Carroll Moran noted the defendants had changed their pleas to guilty during the trial and also accepted that there was no attempt to kill.

While the ongoing feud and various activities of both the Keane and Ryan gangs continued to keep gardaí busy, a third criminal gang, the McCarthy/Dundons had emerged from the shadows and used the cover of the city's main criminal rivalry to establish themselves as a ruthless outfit which would soon become the most dangerous and feared criminal mob in the country. This gang included some of the city's most violent criminals, who would later gain control over the majority of the region's drugs trade.

Kenneth Dundon was born in 1957 and grew up in the Southill area. He met his future wife, Anne McCarthy, in 1971. Anne was from a large family who grew up on the southside of Limerick. In 1974 Kenneth Dundon earned his first conviction for assault in Limerick and served a two-year sentence for wounding with intent. The couple emigrated to London in the 1970s and married in Hackney in 1982, bringing up six children with twelve years between the youngest and oldest. Four of the couples' sons, Wayne, John, Dessie and Gerard were born in England, but would gain notoriety through their activities in Limerick.

Kenneth's first British conviction was for assault occasioning actual bodily harm in 1982 and he was given probation for a similar offence in 1997. He returned to Ireland and narrowly escaped with his life in 1990 when he was shot several times in Limerick. A man was charged with the offence, but the case was dismissed when Dundon failed to show up for the trial in 1993 in Dublin's Central Criminal Court.

However, it is four of Kenneth Dundon's sons who have caused immeasurable grief and anguish for the southside community of Ballinacurra Weston and have led to countless Garda investigations in Limerick and across the country.

Eldest son, eighteen-year-old Wayne followed in his father's footsteps and became involved in serious crime in London and received a four-year sentence for an aggravated burglary, in which he held down a man in a wheelchair while his home was robbed. Wayne was deemed so violent that the Home Office later served him with a deportation order.

The Dundon family returned to Limerick at the turn of the Millennium and linked up with their cousins, the McCarthys. Larry McCarthy junior, who turned twenty-two in 2000, was leading the McCarthy side of the family. In 1999 he received a suspended six-year sentence after conviction on a charge of violent disorder. Larry McCarthy quickly set about forming a formidable alliance with his cousins.

The pairing of the McCarthy and Dundon families would have repercussions for years to come. In September 2000, gardaí investigating the theft of horses from a circus called to the Dundons' home and were immediately greeted with a hail of missiles, including the concrete cap of a pillar and a bag of hardened cement. One of the officers left the force as a result of injuries he sustained.

Wayne Dundon had received a conviction for threatening to smash a prison officer's face in a public toilet of a Limerick shopping centre. The gang became involved in a series of localised feuds on the southside of the city, leading to shootings, arson attacks and attempts to pervert justice. From their bases along Hyde Road, they began to build a tight network around the southside estate of Prospect and Ballinacurra Weston which remains their stronghold to this day.

The gang are believed to be responsible for the vicious sub-machine gun attack on city criminal twenty-seven-year-old John Creamer in 2001. Originally from Southill, Creamer was a ruthless killer who almost died in 1995. He was left on a life-support machine after an assault in Wickham Street in the city, but refused to identify his attackers. Creamer was also at the centre of a murder probe when he was accused of the murder of twenty-six-year-old money-lender John Keane, who was gunned down on July 7, 1996, at his home in O'Malley Park, Southill. The charges were dropped in June 2001 after the guard who arrested Creamer died in a traffic accident. Following an armed robbery of a jewellers in October 2001, Creamer was hit fifteen times when an assailant, armed with a machine gun, opened fire at him at the junction of Hyde Road and Lenihan Avenue in the heart of the McCarthy/Dundon territory around 8pm on October 11. It is believed Creamer has been on his way to collect his share of the haul from the jewellery raid. He was shot in the head, neck, chest, arm, leg and one bullet missed his heart by inches. He suffered twenty-eight entry and exit wounds.

Creamer was rushed to the Mid-Western Regional Hospital and was on the operating table for twelve hours as doctors sought to save his life. Following six operations, he battled for his life for days afterwards. Amazingly, he somehow survived the shooting.

'I was going to visit my uncle Kenneth Dundon, and the shooting happened near his house. I don't have a clue who did it,' Creamer said from his hospital bed a month after the attack.

When the wounded man had first seen the gunman, he had thought it was a joke. 'Then he fired and I hit the deck. I tried to get up but couldn't. He kept firing and was only about ten feet away from me. I collapsed. I was conscious through it all.' Creamer added that he would like to keep one of the bullets recovered from his wounds 'on a chain'.

It is believed that while recovering from the shooting, Creamer was visited by members of the gang and, when he was discharged from hospital, he fled to south Tipperary.

The attack by members of the McCarthy/Dundons on Creamer displayed how they could turn on one of their own associates, without warning. Loyalties to an outfit in Limerick are often decided by fear or intimidation and there is clear evidence of criminals falling out with each other throughout the years.

Since the Dundons return from London, they had linked up with their relations, the McCarthys, and the gang began to exercise greater influence on the city's drug scene. Gardaí attributed rising gun crime to the gang flexing their muscle. While the Keane/Collopy dispute with the Ryans dominated the headlines in the years after Eddie Ryan's death, the activities of this third emerging outfit had not gone unnoticed.

The gang established joint connections with a businessman, who is responsible for the importation of major amounts of drugs to the Munster region through his international contacts, and a Limerick publican, who made his home and property available for the gang's uses. In 2002 the two men were arrested in Manchester with an amount of stolen computer components, but no charges were brought against them.

Dealing on a daily basis with the city's convicted criminals, prison officers were in the front line and often found themselves as the unfortunate targets. John Dundon was jailed for twenty months for threatening to burn down a prison officer's home in August 2001. Wayne Dundon has a conviction relating to threatening a prison officer in a public toilet of a Limerick shopping centre. In January 2002 gunshots were discharged outside the Dooradoyle home of a prison officer, whose car had been petrol-bombed a fortnight earlier. The same week, another member of the prison staff living on the opposite side of the city had his car vandalised with paint. A hoax bomb was also left on the bonnet of a prison officer's car in Ennis, and a second more elaborate suspect package, which had to be made safe by the army's Explosive Ordnance Disposal team, was left outside the home of another in Limerick City.

In March 2002 a courier for the McCarthy/Dundon gang, fifty-six-year-old grandmother, Ann Keane, from Southill, was arrested in the Janesboro area of the city with cocaine and ecstasy worth €32,000. A handgun was also found in her car. When officers searched her rented cottage in a rural area near Rear Cross, County Tipperary, they uncovered a massive drugs distribution centre with cocaine and ecstasy worth €500,000. They also found a ledger in the house, which detailed drugs transactions worth several millions euros for a period covering a few months. Fifteen-year old Ger Dundon, who was acting as courier, was also arrested as part of the operation along with twenty-six-year-old Brian Ahern, Ann Keane's partner. Ann Keane was eventually sentenced to six years' imprisonment in 2003, while Ahern got three years. Ger Dundon received a three years' suspended sentence in April 2004. However, the sentence was activated in October 2005 when he committed three breaches of the public order act and broke his bond to keep the peace for three years. One of the breaches was committed in 2004 when he jeered and roared outside the home of Owen Treacy in St Mary's Park.

Disturbingly for authorities, the McCarthy/Dundons had

dealings with both the Ryan and Collopy outfits following their return to Limerick, but it was their role in two separate incidents which showed how the problem in Limerick had mushroomed beyond all recognition in the space of a small few years.

Doc's nightclub was a well-known nightclub in Limerick. By the end of 2002, it was a popular spot with eighteen- to twenty-three-year-olds and was a favourite haunt of the city's student population.

It was here that married father-of-two, thirty-four-year-old Brian Fitzgerald, worked. Born in Limerick City, he grew up in St Munchin's Street, St Mary's Park, before moving to the nearby Lee Estate in 1980. Brian had two brothers: Martin and Ger, and two sisters: Susan and Breda. He was educated at St Mary's Infant's School, St Senan's CBS, and the Technical Institute, before he started eleven years' employment in Krups on the city's southside. The factory subsequently closed, and Fitzgerald, a sportsman with a strong build, began working as a doorman in city pubs, including the Newtown Pery, before moving to Doc's Bar and nightclub in 1998.

His relationship with his future wife, Alice, was formed in their teenage years, and they had two sons, Aaron and Evan. As he worked nights, the loving father was able to spend a lot of time during the day with his family. The father and his son, Aaron, were often spotted feeding ducks near their home on the Mill Road. In 1996 he received the honour of being asked to tog out for the Munster rugby team for a trial, due to his strong performance for St Mary's

RFC. His physique, after years of bodybuilding and power lifting, made him a natural for the game. Such was his physical presence, teammates and friends asked Brian for advice on training routines and diets.

He also kept two pitbull terriers and was planning to breed pups. Residents in Corbally recalled that, on most evenings, he could be seen walking his dogs on the Mill Road.

He was employed as a security manager at Doc's nightclub, where he was described as being strict but fair to all. Former staff at the nightclub maintained that, while Brian was there, not only did the patrons feel safe, but the rest of his work colleagues did too.

He also encouraged his colleagues to attend work social events. At the last Christmas party he attended in 2001, Brian, complete with a red wig and tartan kilt, took to the stage with his wife, Alice, to perform a duet on the Karaoke machine. After the performance, it was joked by his family that although he had many talents, singing was not one of his gifts.

A close friend of the Fitzgerald family had this to say of the man: 'Brian was a courageous, honourable yet modest man. He had tremendous strength of character and was a natural leader. Brian was a gentle giant. Inside the tough exterior, there was a loving, caring person, who people turned to for guidance and help. Despite his size and strength, he showed respect for everyone he met, and people respected and trusted him. He loved life's simple pleasures: his family, working out at the gym and his dogs.

Brian Fitz' was a one-off. He was a big man with a big reputation and an even bigger heart.'

However, Brian Fitzgerald became a marked man when
he refused to allow drug dealers access to the nightclub. He
was threatened by a leading member of a gang in the city
for this refusal, and the security manager reported this
threat to gardaí. The young criminal behind the threat based
himself in London and Limerick, and already had a suspended prison sentence hanging over him and had been
bound to the peace at a previous court case. If Fitzgerald
testified in court to the threat he had received, the suspended prison sentence hanging over the
twenty-four-year-old would be reactivated, and the emerging drugs boss had no intention of facing a life behind bars.

On the night of November 28, 2002, Brian Fitzgerald
returned to work after a couple of days off. He bathed the
couple's two sons – aged one and five – and stayed with the
children until they fell asleep, before he left for Doc's nightclub at 8.10pm. After feeding one of their children after
2am, Alice stayed up, waiting for her husband to return
home. Brian left work shortly after 3am and dropped colleagues home. At 3.50am, Alice heard her husband's jeep
pulling into the driveway. Unknown to either Brian or Alice,
two men were hiding in nearby bushes: James Martin Cahill
and his teenage accomplice.

Twenty-eight-year-old James Martin Cahill was a fat,
bald, English man, who had been in trouble most of his life.
From Highfield Lane, Quintan, Birmingham, he had family
links in west Clare, but also had a disturbing history. He was

expelled from secondary school for throwing a teacher down a stairs and was no stranger to the law, or the courts, on either side of the Irish Sea. He became a petty criminal in the 1990s and appeared before Birmingham's magistrate courts six times between 1992 and 1997, where he received convictions for criminal damage, wounding, twice interfering with a motor vehicle and theft from a car. He soon earned a reputation as a criminal in Ireland and was convicted of larceny, burglary and criminal damage in 1993, and assault in 1999. Cahill was armed with a 9mm semi-automatic pistol.

With Cahill was a nineteen-year-old from Moyross. Although still in his teenage years, the mention of this individual's surname struck fear into many in Limerick.

James Martin Cahill saw Fitzgerald emerging from his jeep and jumped up from the bushes. Wearing a motorcycle helmet, Cahill opened fire on Fitzgerald. Brian roared at his assailant, 'Come on, ye cunts.' As Alice came downstairs, she heard four gunshots and the sound of breaking glass. The terrified wife saw Brian struggling with the man wearing a motorcycle helmet through the front door. Alice looked in desperation at her husband through the glass panel. With Brian fighting for his life, she raced upstairs to phone the guards for help, but could not get her mobile phone to work and ran downstairs to use the house phone. Fitzgerald, bleeding from a gunshot wound, attempted to flee, but Cahill shot him again across the bonnet of a neighbour's car. The gunman then coldly walked up to Fitzgerald as he lay on the ground and shot him at close range in the head. Cahill fled from the murder scene on a motorbike driven by his teenage accomplice.

The first guard on the scene found Brian's body in a doorway, six doors from his home, around 4.30am. The officer found him lying on his stomach with gunshots wounds to his back and his head and tried to resuscitate him, but Brian Fitzgerald was pronounced dead at 4.55am by a local doctor.

It was a carefully premeditated and planned murder.

Fitzgerald's death immediately led to calls for new legislation to deal with gangland criminals. It was feared that the city's criminals were brazenly attempting to take on law and order in Limerick, and Fitzgerald's murder was a clear statement of their intent.

In a public display of unity and outrage at the spate of violence in Limerick, a silent peace march was attended by hundreds in the city, the week before Christmas 2002.

Fitzgerald was the sixteenth person to die in violent circumstances in the city since March of 2001, and the candlelit march was Limerick's way of publicly rejecting violence in the wake of the latest atrocity. While the brutal death of Fitzgerald three weeks previously was the sad catalyst for the march, organisers of the event, along with members of Brian Fitzgerald's family, stressed it was held in solidarity with everyone in the city who suffered through violence in recent years.

'The reason we are all here tonight is to let people know that we have had enough of violence in Limerick and I am not just talking about what we [his family] suffered,' said

Brian's brother Ger. 'Violence cannot be allowed to continue. It is happening too often and something needs to be done, but we appreciate it won't be done overnight,' he added.

The silent march commenced at Arthur's Quay and continued along O'Connell Street, back down Henry Street to finish at City Hall. Among those who spoke were Nicky Hogan, President of St Mary's RFC – Brian Fitzgerald's rugby club; Mayor of Limerick, John Cronin; organiser Una Heaton and Fr Liam Ryan (OSA). Also present was Anne McCabe, wife of the late Detective Jerry McCabe, who was gunned down by the IRA in Adare in June 1996.

However, a fortnight after the peace march, there was another outrageous murder. Thirty-nine-year-old Sean Poland worked as a part-time car salesman and block-layer. Along with his partner, forty-two-year-old Joanne Lyons, Sean spent New Year's Eve 2002 socialising in Limerick City, before the couple returned to his home at Blackwater, Ardnacrusha, County Clare around 11.30pm.

He had sold a used car for less than €1,000 earlier that week. Unknown to him, the car had been sold to a gang member, and the outfit had decided to pay Sean a visit, to recoup their cash. They were accompanied by a member of a notorious crime family from the city's northside. Poland was shot and died from a single shotgun wound to the lower abdomen when he answered the door of his bungalow to the gang. The culprits stepped over his body in the hallway and subjected his partner, Joanne, to a frightening ordeal as they ransacked the home for cash. Joanne Lyons was tied up, but managed to free herself after the gang left and raised the alarm at a neighbour's house. More than twenty-five people were arrested and questioned, but nobody has been charged with Poland's murder.

The murders of Fitzgerald and Poland left the region in a complete state of shock in the first few days of 2003. But darker days lay ahead. The city's gangs were about to go at each other's throats in such a manner that the entire country stopped and began to take stock of the events which would gain Limerick unwanted worldwide notoriety. A horrific series of incidents were about to take place which displayed that the McCarthy/Dundon's appetite for violence appeared to have no boundaries and that the gang would stop at nothing in pursuit of their vicious objectives.

6

The Feud Erupts

It is common knowledge in Limerick that the Keanes and Ryan gangs liked to dispense their own form of justice and paid no heed to gardaí, the courts or authority. Often after a violent attack, the victims would not even bother to alert gardaí as to what had happened. They would directly sort out the matter themselves with no need for what they regarded as the interference of a third party. The second generation involved in the feud clearly observed a strict obedience to this policy.

On January 23, 2003, Judge Carroll Moran warned that society was in danger of descending into a state of anarchy after another case collapsed in Limerick Circuit Criminal Court when the key witness in a serious assault case, Liam Keane, said he could no longer identify the person he had previously claimed had stabbed him.

Eighteen-year-old Liam – the son of Christy Keane – was giving evidence in a case against nineteen-year-old Kieran 'Rashers' Ryan, the son of murdered Eddie Ryan. Ryan from Hogan Avenue, Kileely, was charged with assault and two counts of being in possession and producing a knife on March 5, 2002, in the city centre. Prosecuting on behalf of the State, barrister John O'Sullivan said Keane had identified the accused man in a statement made to gardaí, but was unable to do so in court. When called to give evidence, Keane told the court that he was stabbed in the back while walking down O'Connell Street.

However, when asked to identify his assailant, Keane replied, 'Kieran Ryan stabbed me in the back. I know his name, but he's not in court.'

Mr O'Sullivan said he could not continue with the case, resulting in Judge Moran directing the jury to find Kieran Ryan not guilty.

The court also heard that Rashers was assaulted by a gang of young men on his way to court shortly before 11am that morning and the legal proceedings were delayed by three hours as a result.

Rashers, left the court and returned to the northside, but the city's underworld had already planned the next course of events. That night, an intricate saga began that was played out over the course of a week, leading to a bloody and violent end.

With Christy Keane locked up and out of the way, the McCarthy/Dundons saw this as their opportunity to gain control of the Limerick drugs trade. The gang from the city's southside teamed up with Eddie Ryan's former associates and his sons. The McCarthy/Dundon gang wanted to take out the main players in the Keane/Collopy alliance, allowing them a monopoly on the drugs market, while Eddie's cronies were seeking revenge for his murder. The McCarthy/Dundons and Ryans staged a devious double-cross on the Keane and Collopys.

On the night the Liam Keane stabbing court case collapsed, gardaí were informed by Sean 'Cowboy' Hanley that Rashers, accompanied by his older brother, twenty-year-old Eddie Ryan Junior, and friend, Christopher 'Smokey' Costelloe, were walking along Moylish Road, Ballynanty, at 11.30pm when a black van pulled up alongside them and the brothers were allegedly abducted at gunpoint while Smokey managed to run off. Smokey later claimed he had been shot at by the abductors as he escaped on foot. The following morning, Limerick awoke to one its biggest ever searches as the Ryan brothers were declared missing.

It appeared as if the young men had disappeared without a trace, and gardaí began investigating the theory that a maze of roads into the neighbouring Clare countryside was used by the abductors as an escape route. Over the course of the next week, gardaí, supported by the army, combed the upland hills of Cratloe Woods, Woodcock Hill and the surrounding regions. No ransom calls were made to the Ryan clan and not a trace of the brothers could be found. Their mother, Mary, and uncle, John Ryan, blamed their rivals in the Island Field for the boys' abduction.

The distraught mother declared to the media, 'They

killed my husband [Eddie]. ... I want my boys back, please give me my boys back ... I never wanted this bloodshed.'

The silence from the Keane/Collopy gang was ominous, and it was feared that the brothers had been murdered and their bodies dumped.

As the search for the brothers entered its fourth day, their uncle, John Ryan, was taunted by members of the opposing side and a fracas developed which involved fifteen people outside the district court on January 27, at 11.45am. Seven were arrested during the melee, some were wearing bullet-proof jackets. Another fight took place in a school yard as tensions mounted. As days of fruitless searches passed by, gardaí privately admitted they were looking for bodies. Suspiciously, on January 28, almost a week after the two siblings disappeared, their close friend Smokey Costelloe, going against the general belief, said he believed he would see his friends again, alive not dead. What the close friends of the brothers knew was that neither brother had been abducted and that they were hiding out in a mobile home near Thurles, County Tipperary.

Throughout the 'abduction saga', members of the Keane/Collopy gang were stopped and questioned regularly by gardaí. No information was gained, but, in truth, the 'Island Field' mob could shed no light on the brothers' disappearance. They had no involvement and were not aware that it was all part of an intricate set up by the McCarthy/Dundon gang. The ruthless gang, along with Eddie Ryan's former associates, decided it was time to take out the main opposition: Kieran Keane and his nephew,

Owen Treacy, along with Philip Collopy. The 'abduction saga' took a sinister turn on Wednesday, January 29, 2003.

With Christy Keane jailed for ten years in 2002, his younger brother, thirty-six-year-old Kieran Keane, had assumed control of the Keane enterprise. Kieran returned to his lavish home in Garryowen on Wednesday afternoon, January 29, 2003, with his wife, Sophie, having collected their two sons from school. Sophie later recalled seeing twenty-year-old Dessie Dundon standing near the Keane Garryowen home, eating a burger. She and her children went into the house as Kieran and Dessie, who both knew each other, spoke briefly for two minutes. Dessie left the area, and Kieran came into the home, ate his dinner, and then he too left, around 4pm, in his 2002-registered, blue Volkswagen Passat.

He proceeded to collect a well-known criminal from St Mary's Park and they made their way to the home of Keane's sister, Pauline (mother of Owen Treacy), in County Clare, and stayed there for a short while before leaving. Keane and his nephew had a lot in common. They both owned horses, Keane had eight, Owen Treacy owned up to fourteen, and both men were often seen in each other's company. As they drove on towards an arranged meeting point, Keane's Passat, which was well known to gardaí, was spotted by a patrol car but soon disappeared. Sophie phoned her husband and he returned the call at 7pm – it was the last time the pair would speak.

Unwittingly, Kieran Keane and his nephew were being lured into a trap. Keane believed that the McCarthy/

Dundons were holding the Ryan brothers. He had been told that if the correct sum, €60,000, was paid, the Ryans would be got rid of.

Acting on this information, Kieran Keane and Owen Treacy arrived at the arranged meeting in a house at Fair-green, Garryowen. Here two twenty-year-old cousins from the McCarthy/Dundon gang, Anthony 'Noddy' McCarthy and Dessie Dundon were lying in wait for them. Keane had dealings with the two in the past and had no reason to fear meeting them. It was the Ryans who posed a constant threat; he was always afraid they would come after him to avenge their father's murder. Keane parked the blue Passat carefully, to avoid being spotted by a passing patrol car, and a man, described in court as Mr X, came to meet them and informed Keane 'the lads were inside.'

The uncle and nephew entered the house, and waiting inside the sitting room for the pair were Dessie Dundon and Noddy McCarthy. Noddy was armed with a handgun. Treacy described the gun as being five to six inches in size, had a spent chamber on it and was like a '38 revolver'.

To their horror, Keane and Treacy realised they were not there on the basis of the pre-arranged meeting. The trap was sprung, and the intent of the McCarthy/Dundon gang became all too clear to Treacy. The two were instructed to sit down, 'play along and ... they would be ok.' They were told to ring Kieran and Philip Collopy, and get them to come out to the Sandwell bank. They refused and Treacy said, 'If me or my uncle made that call, there was four of us going to be killed.'

Their jackets were taken off and they had their hands tied together behind their backs with duct tape by Dessie Dundon. Two men wearing balaclavas appeared from the kitchen area and, despite their balaclavas, Treacy could identify one of the men as thirty-one-year-old David 'Frog Eyes' Stanners. Keane and Treacy continued to refuse repeated demands to get the Collopys to come to a meeting point. Hoods, made up of a net-type material, were then placed over their heads. The pair were brought out of the house and instructed to get into the boot of a silver Nissan Micra. The space in the boot was so cramped that the dividing-shelf had to be removed. Through his hood, Treacy could see Mr X in the passenger seat with Noddy McCarthy driving.

Peering out a side window, Treacy picked out landmarks and knew they were being driven along Bengal Terrace, around a roundabout, towards the Roxboro roundabout, where he could see blue railings. He also noticed a big blue sign outside the old Krups factory. They were taken to a house in Roundwood, Rosbrien, and the small car was parked in the garage of the building, which had been idle for a number of months and to which Mr X had access. Dundon, who arrived separately, took the two from the car and they were brought upstairs where their hoods were removed.

Realising the grim situation they were in, Treacy attempted to leave evidence to show that he had been in the house. He asked Mr X for a glass of water, not to drink but to leave his fingerprints on it. The request was turned down as the water supply was turned off. Treacy and Keane were brought back down the stairs and outside to a waiting 1996 Dublin-registered, green Hiace van and put in the back. Here, Smokey Costelloe – now armed with the same gun that Treacy believed Noddy McCarthy had earlier on – sat with the two abductees in the back while Frog Eyes Stanners drove with a fifth man, twenty-three-year-old James McCarthy, in the front seat.

Terrified for his life, Treacy used every survival instinct available to him and attempted to cut the tape, using a timber panel behind him, to free his hands. However, when he finally succeeded in loosening his hands, the van came to a sudden halt on a dark and quiet road at Drombanna.

Frog Eyes Stanners ordered the uncle and nephew out. Their time had come. Keane was brought to the front of the van, pushed to the ground, while his hands were still tied behind his back. He was repeatedly stabbed in the side of the head before Frog Eyes Stanners lifted the gun, pointed it and shot him in the back of his skull.

'I witnessed David 'Frog Eyes' Stanners shoot my uncle in the back of the head,' Treacy later said.

Kieran Keane had been lured by the McCarthy/Dundon gang on false pretences and paid the ultimate price.

The gun used was the same firearm Smokey Costelloe had in the back of the van. Frog Eyes Stanners left Keane's body lying where he fell and approached Treacy. It was time to get rid of the other man.

'Smokey Costelloe went to stab me in the throat. I grabbed the knife and cut the palm of my hand. Frog Eyes

Stanners took that knife from Christopher 'Smokey' Costelloe and started stabbing me nearly to death,' Treacy
recalled.

As his screams pierced the cold country air, Treacy was
stabbed seventeen times in the upper body, in the chest,
around his neck and ears; one thrust penetrated right into
his lung with terrible force and pressure.

'This is the last face you are going to see,' Frog Eyes said
to Treacy, during the frenzied assault.

The St Mary's Park man had looked for an escape route
throughout the entire ordeal and, instinctively, he lay
motionless on the cold road, playing dead, fervently hoping
that his abductors would believe they had finished him off.

The bait was taken. James McCarthy shouted, 'He's dead,
he's dead, he's dead!'

The van left and Treacy hauled himself to his feet. He
went over to his uncle, but could do nothing as Keane had
suffered six stab wounds to the head and was shot dead at
point-blank range. With blood pouring from his body,
Treacy began to stagger along the road but spotted lights
approaching him and jumped into a ditch, fearing it was
'the boys' coming back to finish him off. When the passing
vehicle went by, he got up and made it as far as a house
with big gates and a buzzer. No one answered and he
fought his way up the road to another house, where he
rang the bell. A child no older than seven opened the door
to see Owen Treacy standing in front of him covered in
blood from head to toe.

In the meantime, Sophie Keane had attempted to call her

husband, Kieran, up to fifteen times between 8 and 9.15pm and sent numerous text messages, to no avail. Worried about his whereabouts, Sophie called to Owen Treacy's wife, Donna, and telephoned gardaí to alert them that the two men were missing. Along with Kieran's brother, Anthony, she searched the Fairgreen area of the city for the missing men.

By the time, gardaí were alerted at 9.30pm, the six responsible for the abduction were making their escape. Treacy had been rushed to the Mid-Western Hospital.

That night, gardaí stopped a Volvo car travelling to Dublin near Roscrea, County Tipperary. Inside the car were Anthony 'Noddy' McCarthy, Dessie Dundon and Mr X, who had not made the trip to Drombanna. All supplied officers with false names, including that of Jim 'Chaser' O'Brien. Evidence was later supplied in court that the Volvo car was registered to Jim 'Chaser' O'Brien's former pub, 'The Chaser's' in Pallasgreen (the pub has since changed hands).

Sophie Keane identified her husband's remains in the morgue of the Mid-Western Regional Hospital.

Within hours of Keane's murder, Eddie Junior and Rashers Ryan made a phone call to Portlaoise Garda station, declaring they were alive and well and were immediately located by officers. The most sinister and detailed plot, to date, in the feud had just been played out, but the exact sequence of events would not become clear for a number of months. The two brothers were brought from the midlands immediately to Henry Street Garda station, where they were united with their tearful mother after 5am. The clean-shaven brothers revealed little to gardaí initially and said they were kept in a caravan and fed on takeaway food once a day.

Within hours, a major party was taking place at the Ryan home in Kileely to celebrate the brothers' homecoming, while across the river in St Mary's Park, the Keane family were grieving the murder of Kieran. There could not have been more contrasting scenes between the feuding sides in the city that day. In Kileely, bottles of beer and alcopops were passed about freely at the Ryan home, and one associate of the brothers even mooned at the posse of photographers and cameramen gathered outside the terraced house.

Rashers Ryan said he was just happy to be home. 'I am going to get drunk and celebrate. I got threatened and I am not going to talk to no one about it,' he told reporters.

Rashers' uncle, John Ryan, told Eugene Hogan of the *Irish Independent* in 2003 that his family had nothing to do with the murder of Kieran Keane, 'We had no involvement in that last night. It was their own doing last night. Whether there was somebody else interfering and shot them we don't know. We didn't do it anyway. My house has been shot thirty times. They have tormented us. We do want an end to it. They started the whole lot off again and they are after pushing us too far. We don't want any trouble. We want no revenge now. Everything is sorted out now. But if they continue on again, we will start again.'

Less than twelve hours after he assisted in the murder of Keane, James McCarthy was pictured outside the Ryan household, celebrating the brothers' homecoming. When asked, at the time, if he felt the return of the Ryan brothers and Kieran Keane's death were in any way linked, he gave a flat and instant denial.

Across the city, in St Mary's Park, armed gardaí and the Emergency Response Unit (ERU) attempted to prevent heightened tensions from boiling over onto the street and across the river towards the Ryans. The thirst for revenge hung heavy in the air. Parents quickly escorted their children to and from school as they tried to get on with their family lives in an environment which resembled an estate under siege, ravaged by fear and tension. Gardaí equipped with bulletproof vests patrolled the Island Field, and all vehicles entering the estate were stopped and checked. An unfamiliar face in the area was regarded with deep suspicion. From the events to date, experience had taught those living in St Mary's Park that it would not be long before another atrocity occurred. At the time, Martin Scorsese's *Gangs of New York* was attracting record viewers to the country's cinemas, but, in reality, it was the gangs of Limerick which held the country gripped with a morbid fascination.

Irish Independent reporter Eugene Hogan soon learned whom the St Mary's Park gang blamed for Keane's murder as they issued a chilling warning to the Ryans and their associates. In a thinly disguised, sarcastic threat, Keane's associates said that they would like to celebrate the release of Kieran and Eddie Ryan with a drink, and the 'shots' would be on them.

Meanwhile, Owen Treacy was receiving intensive treatment at the Mid-Western Regional Hospital, where he was afforded round-the-clock armed protection.

Commissioner Patrick Byrne and Deputy Commissioner Noel Conroy provided a full briefing on the latest developments in Limerick to Justice Minister, Michael McDowell.

Living alongside the Keane gang and cut off from the rest of his outfit, John Ryan boarded up his Lee Estate home with protective steel shutters and fled the house within two days of Keane's murder as fears of reprisal attacks grew. Members of the Ryan and McCarthy/Dundon gang, including one of Keane's murderers, fled to the UK as the massive Garda investigation swung into action.

The retaliation attacks soon began. Three days after Keane's murder, the first reprisal took place when a home belonging to a woman connected to the two Ryan brothers was petrol-bombed in Lee Estate. On February 5, in freezing rain, 800 people attended Keane's removal in the city centre. At 7am, the following morning, a house belonging to the McCarthy/Dundon gang on Hyde Road was hit in an arson attack. Quickly, it was becoming clear that the McCarthy/Dundon gang had been the orchestrators behind the abduction and murder of Keane.

The dead man's brother, convicted drug dealer Christy, was refused temporary release from prison to attend Kieran Keane's funeral, but Owen Treacy had recovered sufficiently enough to attend. Just over 400 mourners attended the funeral mass at St Mary's Church and the burial afterwards at Kilmurry cemetery in Castletroy.

Fr Donough O'Malley consoled Keane's widow, Sophie, and her sons, Joseph and Kieran Junior. The priest begged mourners to turn towards peace and not to seek revenge. Two hearses brought the large collection of floral tributes reading, 'No 1 Dad' and 'Our Pal' to the burial ground. For safety journalists and photographers kept their distance from the cortege.

The investigation into the murder of Kieran Keane was one of the most intensive ever mounted by gardaí in Limerick. It was clear from the outset that the victim's nephew, Owen Treacy, was going to be an integral part of this process and his evidence would be vital for any possible future prosecutions that the State hoped to bring. Treacy was interviewed by gardaí while recovering in hospital. Over the course of several days, Det Sgt Eamon O'Neill and Det Jerry Doherty carefully pieced together the complex web of what unfolded in the hours before Kieran Keane's murder. Graffiti began to appear in Southill and Prospect, labelling Owen Treacy, the potential State witness, 'a rat'. Treacy was about to break the code of silence amongst the city's criminal gangs and essentially provide the State with the basis for their prosecution.

Whatever about the kidnapping of the two Ryan brothers, the jigsaw regarding the murder of Keane and attempted murder of Treacy soon began to fall into place and, after arresting and questioning almost thirty people, officers pinpointed it down to five men who had all come to their attention before.

Less than two months after the bloody January night,

three men were charged with the false imprisonment of Kieran Keane on March 23, 2003. Christopher 'Smokey' Costelloe from Moylish Avenue, Ballynanty, along with David 'Frog Eyes' Stanners and James McCarthy, both with addresses at Pineview Gardens, Moyross, appeared before Judge Terence Finn for the false imprisonment of the slain crime boss and his nephew. They were met by chants of 'now the game starts' and 'you're finished' by members of the Keane gang as they were escorted, under armed protection, to and from the courthouse. In full view of solicitors, assembled media and gardaí, feuding gang members cocked their fingers in the shape of guns and mouthed the words 'you're next' at each other. On the same weekend as the court sitting, an Uzi sub-machine gun destined for the Limerick feud was recovered by the ERU in Naas while an automatic and sawn-off shotgun and fully loaded automatic pistols were recovered near Moyross.

The three defendants were refused bail by Judge Leo Malone shortly after their initial charge and by the end of March they were joined by two more of their accomplices as gardaí had all five men responsible for the murder of Keane charged and in custody. Noddy McCarthy of Fairgreen, Garryowen, was arrested in Kilkenny on March 28. He had dyed his hair and had returned to the State from the UK. Along with his cousin, Dessie Dundon, from Hyde Road, the two were charged with false imprisonment of the uncle and nephew on March 31.

That summer, all five were charged with the murder of Kieran Keane and attempted murder of Owen Treacy. All the accused had first-hand knowledge of the workings of the district court and were regarded by gardaí across the city as serious criminals.

Smokey Costelloe had appeared before the courts for various charges and was convicted of burglary, criminal damage and assault. He was banned from driving for ten years in 2001. Frog Eyes Stanners had recorded fifteen previous convictions, dating back to the 1980s, including cruelty to an animal. James McCarthy had fourteen convictions, the vast majority for motoring offences, but had also been sentenced to four months in prison for possession of drugs for sale or supply. Dessie Dundon had two convictions relating to the time investigating gardaí were attacked and assaulted at the Dundon home in 2000 and a larceny offence. Noddy McCarthy had amassed nine previous convictions, including public order and drug offences and the assault of a prison officer.

A massive book of evidence comprising of 5,000 pages with 720 sworn statements was served on each of the five men as the opening of one of the most eagerly anticipated criminal trials in the history of the State drew closer. Mr Justice Paul Carney ruled in the Central Criminal Court that the men must stand trial in Limerick where they would be tried before a Limerick jury, despite an application to have the trial moved to Dublin. The security and logistics employed at the Limerick courthouse for the calling of the trial in October 2003 were unprecedented and at enormous cost. Crowd-control barriers were erected on all approach routes to the building and all persons entering, including potential jurors, were searched for weapons or suspicious items. Sniffer dogs were brought to the building to search for explosives, while a number of Garda snipers were placed on the roof of the court building with other armed members stationed in the grounds of the adjacent St Mary's Cemetery and in the precincts of the court itself. The Garda air unit hovered over the city centre, while a boat from the water unit patrolled the Shannon river. The State's chief witness, Owen Treacy, was brought in amid the same heightened security and taken straight to the public gallery, where he was surrounded by armed officers.

However, it was the problems of assembling a jury and beginning the case that gained the most publicity in the opening days. Initially, it was delayed a day after Mr Justice Paul Carney fell ill and was replaced on the bench by Mr Justice Paul Butler. At the opening day on October 21, 2003, of the 529 potential jurors summoned, the list was whittled down to 170 because of ineligibility and an unusually high proportion of sick notes. Another 70 failed to show up while 90 of the remaining 100 were objected to, or were excused, as they knew one or more of the five accused, the victims or their families. Left with a jury of just ten people rather than the standard twelve from the 529 potential jurors, Mr Justice Butler transferred the trial from Limerick to Dublin on October 24, saying it would be 'lunacy' to try the case with just ten jurors.

Cloverhill courthouse, part of Wheatfield prison, was chosen to hold the trial as the Four Courts building was busy at the time. The trial finally began in early November in front of a jury of seven men and five women.

Mr Justice Paul Carney advised the jury that he could have them placed in a hotel to protect them from the 'activities' of the media throughout the trial. Defence counsels had submitted what they deemed was prejudicial material from the broadcast and print media. The jury was given free vaccinations to protect them from illness if a flu epidemic broke out during the high-profile trial.

On November 7, the atmosphere in the packed courtroom was tense, as Owen Treacy, flanked by two plainclothes gardaí from the Special Protection Unit, gave evidence of what happened on the day his uncle was murdered. His side of affairs was going to be crucial and he proved to be a strong witness, despite having to face the five men that attempted to murder him earlier that year.

The case lasted for thirty-one days, and the State's key witness was subjected to an intense cross-examination in the witness box for eight days. Further evidence was heard of fibres from clothes matching Keane's being found at various locations. Evidence was interrupted as applications to the judge were made and legal argument ensued. Other charges arose from incidents during the trial itself.

On November 13, at Cloverhill court, John Dundon, brother of Dessie, announced to Owen Treacy's wife, Donna, 'I swear on my baby's life when this is over I am going to kill Owen Treacy.' He was subsequently charged and sentenced in January 2005 to four-and-a-half years' imprisonment for the offence of threatening to kill or cause serious harm to the State witness.

The judicial process was moved from Cloverhill to the Four Courts for the jury's deliberations and, on December 20, when the jury indicated they had reached a verdict, after debating for more than fifteen hours over the course of three days, the tension was palpable.

When guilty verdicts were returned on all charges, the five murderers, Anthony 'Noddy' McCarthy, Dessie Dundon, James McCarthy, Christopher 'Smokey' Costelloe and David 'Frog Eyes' Stanners erupted. Noddy McCarthy leapt to his feet and stood on the defendants' bench in the court, ignoring requests by the prison officers and gardaí to sit down. His eyes scanned the watching gallery, seeking out the faces of Sophie Keane and Owen Treacy.

'For every action, there's a reaction, you just remember that,' Noddy McCarthy shouted, staring directly at Treacy before warning him that, 'You'll be looking over your shoulder for the rest of your life.'

When order was restored, Sophie Keane was called to the evidence box and told Judge Paul Carney the effect the murder had on her life and that of her two teenage sons.

'Our lives have stopped moving forward. These men are animals. They took my husband's life for no reason. He never did anybody any harm,' the widow said.

When asked what her husband worked at, the five again started shouting, before she had the chance to answer. 'Selling drugs, killing people. He killed the McCarthys, he killed Eddie Ryan,' they roared.

Sophie's eventual answer that her husband 'sold coal' brought guffaws and laughter from the five convicted men.

Outside the court, Treacy, whose evidence had jailed the men for life, said, 'They got what they deserved.'

The curtain on one of the biggest trials in the history of the State came down, in February 2004, when the five men were brought to Limerick courthouse, and Mr Justice Paul Carney issued a dire warning: 'I want to say primarily to the friends and supporters of the accused on the outside that they and each of them [the accused] will die in prison, unless in the fullness of time there is an intervention in their cases by the Parole Board. It is an entirely independent board and it seems to me unlikely to intervene while the feud is a live issue. That should be borne in mind by the supporters on the outside as well as the accused them-selves.'

Supt Gerry Mahon said the prime motivation for the feud was 'sheer and absolute hate' by each side for each other, which had not diminished since they were found guilty of the murder. He told the court: 'The motivation and objective was to murder Kieran Keane and Owen Treacy, and to lure two other people into a trap from which, I believe, two other murders would occur had they been successful. It [the hit] was to eliminate all that would stand in their way and those perceived to be their enemies with the objective of totally dominating Limerick City.'

Less than half an hour after the conclusion of the case, the very same people, for whom Judge Carney's warning was intended, were still openly flaunting the type of unre-lenting revulsion for their rivals that has typified the feud. As a group of around thirty supporters of the five men

Burnt-out cars in Moyross in November 2000.

Delmege Park, Moyross.

Eddie Ryan.

Christy Keane.

Eddie Ryan's funeral on November 16, 2000.

Kieran Keane.

Sophie Keane.

Liam Keane.

Eddie Ryan Junior, Mary Ryan and Kieran 'Rashers' Ryan
outside their home in Kileely on January 30, 2003.

David 'Frog Eyes' Stanners.

Christopher 'Smokey' Costelloe.

Armed garda at Limerick courthouse in July 2008.

Supporters of McCarthy/Dundon gang, wearing T-shirts at the sentencing of Kieran Keane's murderers at Limerick Court in February 2004.

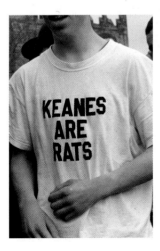

Armed garda in Limerick on April 11, 2008.

Drugs, firearms and ammunition recovered during Operation Anvil on June 30, 2006.

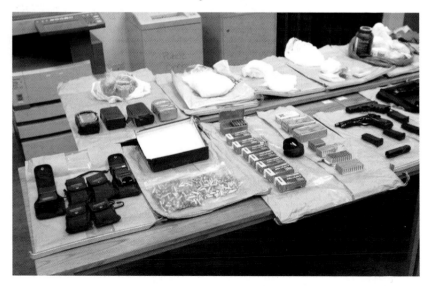

Anthony Kelly.

John Ryan.

The murder scene following John Ryan's shooting on July 7, 2003.

Millie and Gavin Murray with their mother Sheila.

Pineview Gardens, Moyross.

waited outside the courtroom, the chief State witness in the trial and man who effectively put the quintet down, Owen Treacy, emerged to screams of 'you rat' from men, women and teenagers as he was taken away by Garda escort. A youth of no more than sixteen whipped off his top in front of the cameras to proudly display the words 'Keanes are Rats' printed on his T-shirt. A number of young girls waved excitedly at the men as they were led away, and cheers of encouragement and support were roared to the five murderers. In the twisted and brutal world of Limerick's feuding elements, murderers somehow seemed to have acquired iconic status.

The murder of Kieran Keane was clear proof that the McCarthy/Dundons were now intent on grasping control of Limerick's drugs market, and were using the Ryan/Keane feud as their opportunity to do so. Although they had previous dealings with the Keane gang, two of the McCarthy/Dundon's henchmen, Anthony 'Noddy' McCarthy and Dessie Dundon, had managed to lure Keane and Treacy on false pretences and had delivered them into the hands of the associates of the late Eddie Ryan in a treacherous and intricate double-cross. Equally, complicit in the implementation of the joint enterprise were friends of the Ryan brothers, Stanners, Costelloe and James McCarthy. The entire double-cross saga showed the lengths that the now-aligned McCarthy/Dundons and Ryan gangs would go to in their battle against their hated rivals.

7

The Murder Toll
Escalates

Following the brutal slaying of Kieran Keane, public figures, including the then Taoiseach Bertie Ahern, politicians
from all parties, senior gardaí and members of the legal pro-
fession called for restraint. The Bishop of Limerick, Donal
Murray, asked the feuding gangs to desist from violence
and looked for people to pray, so that the 'Prince of Peace'
would be with them and their city. Over the coming
months, the pleas fell on deaf ears.

Throughout 2003 tensions had heightened on Limerick's
gangland scene. Gang members were more determined
than ever to settle old scores. The gardaí found themselves
up against an increasingly highly organised, vicious and
cunning criminal fraternity. The methods and level of planning that went into the Brian Fitzgerald murder and the

Keane/Treacy abduction and murder were testament to this.

The entry of the McCarthy/Dundons, who publicly aligned themselves with the Ryans and were instantly at war with the Keanes, was yet another major problem for under-resourced gardaí.

Despite the fact that Kieran Keane was now out of the picture, and the five men responsible for his killing were arrested and soon to be convicted, there were many others waiting in the wings, eager to step into the breach and fill the void. Those at the top of the criminal chains had no shortage of obedient lieutenants and foot soldiers, willing to carry out their instructions.

At the time of the Kieran Keane murder, Limerick had established itself as the thriving industrial capital of the Mid-West region, attracting major inward investment from around the globe. It was recognised as a modern, progressive city with a strong cultural, social and sporting heartbeat, but was also struggling to stave off its reputation for serious crime. The murder figure continued to rise, and senior gang members dealt ruthlessly with those caught carrying out their dirty work.

Twenty-eight-year-old Philip Deane from Birmingham, England, was arrested on the Dublin Road, Limerick, on January 14, 2003. Gardaí stopped Deane's British-registered Opel Cavalier, believing that he was importing drugs, but Detectives Cora O'Grady and Larry Glavin uncovered a mega-light pocket torch concealed in a duvet in the boot, a handgun and ammunition. The torch had been converted into a firearm capable of discharging a .22 inch calibre round of ammunition. A hole was drilled at the rear of the flashlight where the battery is normally contained and it was fitted with a barrel mechanism. A spring mechanism was also inserted into the torch and when this was pulled and let go, it would discharge a round of ammunition.

Deane was importing weapons for the McCarthy/Dundons from Britain to Ireland and had been warned that he would get a 'bullet in the back of the head', if he did not continue to do so. He was held in solitary confinement at Limerick Prison after his arrest. His partner and two children, aged five and three, had to go into hiding in Britain, after their home was firebombed, days before Deane appeared in court for his sentencing, in April 2003. Deane received a three-year jail sentence when he pleaded guilty to two counts of possession of firearms and a third of possession of ammunition without lawful excuse. In 2007, at a bail application in the High Court, Judge Paul Butler heard that several attempts had been made on Deane's life. Deane was put in the Witness Protection Programme, following his release. Gardaí considered that Deane's life would be at risk as he possessed intimate knowledge of the murder of Brian Fitzgerald and had agreed to co-operate with officers and give evidence.

The arrival of summer and the May bank holiday weekend brought further gangland violence and another attempt on a man's life when Joseph 'Do Do' McCarthy was shot in the chest, at point-blank range, around 10pm, on May 1. Two gunmen had followed their target into the kitchen area of a house at Craeval Park, Moyross, before opening fire on him. Following lifesaving surgery, McCarthy survived the attack.

Five days later, another resident of Moyross was not so lucky. Twenty-three-year-old Robert Fitzgerald, from Cliona Park, was shot dead in the early hours of May 6, as he made his way home from a house party in the area. The gunman lay in wait for Fitzgerald and shot him once in the back in a dark laneway between College Avenue and Cliona Park. The assailant, who was believed to be a local, then stood over Fitzgerald as he lay prostrate on the ground and shot him fatally in the back of the head less than fifty yards from where the house party was taking place. Armed Garda patrols were in the estate at the time.

Fitzgerald was described as a popular man and was raised by his grandmother. Moyross Parish Priest, Fr Frank O'Dea, appealed to the better senses of the community, telling them that violence was not the answer at the young man's funeral. Standing at the altar, Robert Fitzgerald Senior battled to hold back the tears as he paid tribute to his mother, Mary, for rearing his only son. One theory pursued by gardaí was that the hit was the savage settling of a personal grievance the killer had with Fitzgerald. No one was ever charged with Fitzgerald's death and to this day, the exact motive for his murder remains unclear.

Despite the constant presence of gardaí monitoring the activities of the main criminals, it was only a matter of time before the feuding outfits crossed paths again. Tensions amongst the criminal classes were high as the secondary schools prepared to close for the three-month holidays. Noel Price and Michael Stanners had been jailed for twelve years for carrying out the arson attack at the home of Owen Treacy's father, and murder charges were being prepared for the five men in custody for the abduction of Kieran Keane. It was always feared that a large-scale confrontation would take place, if members of the opposing sides came across each other in the same place. This occurred on May 27, 2003, at the car park of Supermac's fast-food restaurant on the Ennis Road.

Three vehicles, containing members of the Garda sub aqua and technical training units, were on convoy from Fermoy, County Cork, to Lahinch, County Clare, when they were passing the busy fast-food restaurant that afternoon. Officers immediately noticed a lot of commotion in the car park with men wielding sticks and other implements and behaving in an aggressive and threatening manner towards each other. One man involved had a bloody injury to his head. Gardaí intervened, called for back-up, separated the brawling parties and recovered a number of improvised weapons, including baby's feeding chairs, pool cues, a steering lock, steel bars, a golf club and a brush. In total, nine men were brought before the courts in relation to the running battle the following year.

When the case was heard in 2004, Limerick Circuit Criminal Court was told that the intervention of passing gardaí in the running battle defused a 'potentially explosive situation'. Five of the accused before the court and aligned to the Ryan side of the feud were twenty-one-year-old Patrick 'Pa'

McCarthy of College Avenue, Moyross; his brother twenty-three-year-old Edward McCarthy of O'Callaghan Avenue, Kileely; twenty-year-old Kieran 'Rashers' Ryan (son of the slain Eddie Ryan) with an address at Pineview Gardens, Moyross; twenty-six-year-old David McCarthy, also from O'Callaghan Avenue, Kileely and nineteen-year-old David Sheehan from Cliona Park, Moyross. They all pleaded not guilty to violent disorder but were found guilty of the offences by a jury, after four hours of deliberations, following a thirteen-day trial.

From the other side of the feud, and all hailing from St Mary's Park, were thirty-seven-year-old Declan 'Darby' Sheehy, St Brendan's Street; brothers, thirty-four-year-old Ray 'Jethro' and twenty-three-year-old Philip Collopy of St Ita's Street and forty-one-year-old Anthony Keane (brother of murdered Kieran) from St Munchin's Street. All four were charged with violent conduct, while two of them, Philip Collopy and Anthony Keane, each pleaded guilty to a charge of possession of offensive weapons.

Eight, of the nine brought before the court, had a collective total of seventy-three previous convictions, with the exception of Ray Collopy who had none and was a member of the Irish angling team and winner of the European Championships in 2001.

Detective Sergeant Eamon O'Neill told Judge Carroll Moran that the genesis of this feud was a falling-out over the sale and supply of drugs in the city in 2000, and that, 'These people are intent since this serious fracture on wiping each other out.'

When passing sentence on the nine men in June 2004, Judge Carroll Moran described the violent Limerick feud as the city's 'most serious problem'. Four of the nine men, Patrick 'Pa' McCarthy, Kieran Ryan, Edward McCarthy and David McCarthy, were each jailed for six years, while David Sheehan was jailed for five years and three months. Raymond Collopy and Declan Sheehy were jailed for two and three years respectively. Philip Collopy and Anthony Keane were both sentenced to two years' imprisonment.

'There is a lot of hype about this problem and some of it is exaggerated and we all appreciate that. But this problem has evolved over the last three to four years as an extremely serious problem and ... it has to stop,' declared Judge Moran.

A week after the Supermac's incident, Kieran Keane's widow, Sophie, found herself in the local district court when the car in which she was travelling rammed a vehicle transporting rival family members near Annacotty on the Dublin Road. Sophie was charged with four breaches of the public order act: two counts of failing to comply with the instructions of a Garda and two of engaging in threatening and abusive language calculated to lead to a breach of the peace. She was bound to the peace for a year, when her solicitor explained she let her 'feelings get the better of her'.

The feud reached another low in late June when rival gang members fought at a graveside, following a burial. Up to five men assaulted a rival with a wheel brace, within minutes of the burial taking place at Mount St Oliver's Cemetery, but all had fled the area by the time gardaí arrived. The woman whose funeral had taken place was not related to either side. Again no complaint was made to gardaí by the injured party.

Only half the year had passed, but already 2003 was quickly transpiring to be an annus horribilis for the city of the Treaty Stone, as an absolute indifference to life spread through Limerick's criminal community like the deadliest of viruses. Unfortunately, there were people willing to exact the highest price possible, that of a life, to settle a minor score.

As the situation continued to worsen, brother of murdered Eddie Ryan, John, called to Willie O'Dea's constituency clinic on the first Saturday in July. John Ryan's plight was well documented before his visit to the government TD. Ryan told the Fianna Fáil TD he urgently needed a new home and expressed his fear of being killed as his family had become open targets in the gang warfare.

At 6.30pm, on July 7, 2003, Ryan's fate was sealed. He was laying a patio at the front of a house in Thomondgate, as traffic moved along the busy High Road. Ryan was working alongside the estate of Kileely and felt safe on the northside of the river. He had placed his jumper on one pier and a jacket on the other. His empty coffee cup and packet of twenty cigarettes were left on the wall. Ryan had spent the day working on the paving, and was easily spotted by anyone travelling or walking by. As Ryan worked on into the evening, less than a half mile away, a full meeting of Limerick City Council was underway at City Hall to elect a new mayor. However, democracy does not come into the pantheon of crime when Limerick's ruthless gangs decide to elect a victim and strike.

A gunman and getaway driver approached Ryan on a motorcycle as he bent to his task. The pillion passenger dismounted and discharged four shots, two of them ripping into Ryan's abdomen and thigh. The two assailants, both wearing motorcycle helmets, escaped in the direction and safety of St Mary's Park immediately after the shooting.

The forty-seven-year-old's injuries initially did not seem to be life threatening. However, by the time he had been rushed to the Mid-West Regional Hospital, it was all too late.

John Ryan's daughter, twenty-year-old Sammy Joe, accompanied her father in the ambulance. She was distraught as she tried to come to terms with her father's death and she told Jimmy Woulfe of the *Evening Echo*: 'They are all scum in the Island Field .... We are left on our own now with no father. I am sick of it. We had to get out of our own house because of it [the feud].'

News of the murder spread across the city like wildfire, and the word on everyone's lips was revenge for the murder of Kieran Keane. Every available off-duty Garda in Limerick was requested to return to work that night.

John Ryan was gunned down as he was a senior public figure of the Ryan family and had spoken out on numerous occasions, making inflammatory comments against the Keanes and issuing veiled threats. After the murder of Kieran Keane, John Ryan was a marked man.

Ryan's nephew, Fat John McCarthy from Cliona Park, Moyross – whose son had narrowly avoided death when their home was shot at in an AK-47 shooting, the previous summer – revealed that he warned his uncle not to work in the Thomondgate area: 'He was an easy target in Thomondgate. I told him lots of times to stay out of the Thomondgate area. It was too risky for him. He was doing work here and there and wasn't expecting nothing. I got a phone call from a friend to say he had been shot and I got down there and saw him being taken away in an ambulance. He wasn't dead at that time. He was pulling the breathing mask off his face. He was talking before he went into the ambulance. I wasn't talking to him myself, but I knew he was breathing. I didn't think then he was that badly injured at all. I came back up home and got a phone call from a relation of mine saying he was dead.'

In a sinister development, Fat John McCarthy also claimed that the rival gang had telephoned one of his friends, after his uncle's murder, to say they were celebrating his death.

'There will be no backing down from them, but we didn't expect this for Johnny,' Fat John said.

Minutes after he was elected the first citizen of Limerick, Mayor Dick Sadlier's first task was to appeal for restraint among the feuding gangs:

'Those people must realise they have no future in violence. On a human level, they must sit down and talk and address their differences. There is no future in this kind of violence. It does not reflect the rest of Limerick and I condemn it and regret it.'

Ironically, the murder of John Ryan happened on the eve

of the historic first sitting of the Central Criminal Court in Limerick. The move of the court to Limerick was designed to free up gardaí from travelling to Dublin for cases, so they could continue to concentrate on crime prevention and detection.

The red motorcycle used in the shooting was discovered in wasteland, in the St Mary's Park area. Investigating officers suspected that two local youths, under the direction of the Keane gang, were responsible for Ryan's murder. Both were arrested and questioned, but no charges were ever brought. The alleged suspects availed of their right to silence and said absolutely nothing to interrogating gardaí. The only man charged in relation to the John Ryan investigation was later cleared by a jury of a charge of failing to disclose information about the whereabouts of the motorbike used in the shooting. Nobody has been charged with the murder to date.

As sure as night follows day, the violence continued in Limerick that year. Three months after the murder of John Ryan, and as the Kieran Keane trial was about to begin, the feud claimed another life. A man walking his dog in Coca Barry's field in Rathbane, Limerick, on the morning of October 20, 2003, discovered a body. He alerted construction workers on the nearby southern ring road, who rang Roxboro gardaí.

Twenty-three-year-old Michael Campbell-McNamara had suffered a brutal death, after he was lured to the city's southside, where he was bound and tortured through stabbings and shootings from the McCarthy/Dundon gang.

The night previously, at 10.45pm, the young man, who was extremely cautious about his movements as it was known he was an associate of the Keane family, received a phone call from a man well known to him – Andrew Nolan of Ashe Avenue, John Carew Park, Southill. Campbell-McNamara was originally from Southill and was looking to equip himself with a gun for protection. He trusted Nolan and the former baker offered him a pump-action shotgun for €700. Campbell-McNamara told a family member that he wanted to buy it and left to drive to Nolan's house. En route, Brian Collopy from St Mary's Park received a phone call from Campbell-McNamara to inform him he was purchasing the firearm. Brian Collopy received another phone call at 1.26am.

'Where are you now? My head is wrecked. Are you in Fedamore? Can I go out and stay with you?' Campbell-McNamara asked.

That was the last time gardaí knew that he was alive. His car was found burning in Fedamore at 2.40am – a few miles from the city.

Andrew Nolan fled the State shortly after the murder, but was arrested when he returned for a birthday party for one of his children on October 7, 2006. He appeared in Limerick Circuit Criminal Court in 2007 and admitted luring Michael Campbell-McNamara to his death. In a statement read out in court, Nolan said two people, who were later joined by another man, called to his home to get Michael Campbell-McNamara to come up there.

'Three men were waiting for him at the shop. I don't

want to name them. I have kids. I don't mind for myself,' Andrew Nolan told investigating officers.

The defendant admitted to gardaí that he knew the unnamed men who requested a meeting with their victim were violent, had access to guns and would kill. Campbell-McNamara was taken away by three men and gardaí suspect they attempted to get him to lure members of the Collopy family from St Mary's Park to a meeting point, but failed to do so.

Later that night, Louise Campbell-McNamara got two phone calls from her brother, asking her to ring another party. She refused, because of the late hour.

Campbell-McNamara's wrists, feet and ankles had been tied together and the Limerick man was shot in the back of the pelvic region and shot in the head with a shotgun. He was then stabbed in the back ten times.

Andrew Nolan, the only man charged in connection with the death, pleaded guilty to engaging in conduct which created a substantial risk of death or serious harm to the victim.

Judge Carroll Moran said it was not the case that the twenty-seven-year-old Andrew Nolan murdered Michael Campbell-McNamara, but 'he lured him in a position where he was brutally killed' and the judge sentenced Nolan to four years' imprisonment, in July 2007.

Throughout 2003, Limerick was rarely outside the national news with the Kieran Keane murder trial in the final two months. However, it was the crime lord's nephew, nineteen-year-old Liam Keane, who found himself on the front pages when a murder case against him collapsed at the Central Criminal Court in Dublin, on November 3. Weeks beforehand, Liam – the son of Christy Keane – had carried the coffin of Michael Campbell-McNamara from the church at his funeral.

Liam Keane was charged with the murder of Tesco worker, nineteen-year-old Eric Leamy, from Lee Estate, on the night of August 28/29, 2001, but in a dramatic set of circumstances, the case collapsed as prosecution witnesses under oath in court denied giving statements to gardaí, incriminating Keane.

Two versions of what happened on the night Eric Leamy died transpired, but the only version that counted took place in court and, according to events there, six witnesses were too drunk or 'stoned' to see anything as he was stabbed to death near his home estate. The prosecution had no option but to enter a verdict of 'nolle prosequi'.

Mr Justice Paul Carney said he had never encountered 'the likes of what happened in this case', and Liam Keane, dressed in a dark suit, walked free from court into the bright sunshine, giving photographers an infamous two-fingered salute. However, the young criminal would find himself before the judicial system on many occasions in years to come.

Subsequently, a number of prosecutions from the collapsed trial were brought forward again, and evidence of the level of intimidation against some of the witnesses was provided in the Circuit Criminal Court in 2007. It was only at the court cases of those prosecuted after the collapsed trial that the intense intimidation and pressure that had been put on some of the witnesses became apparent.

Following a two-day trial, twenty-nine-year-old Roy Behan of Cherrydale Court, on the Dublin Road, was found guilty of committing perjury. Roy Behan had accompanied Eric Leamy to hospital on the night he died and had also carried his coffin at the funeral. On October 31, 2003, while on his way to Dublin for the murder trial, Roy Behan told Eric Leamy's parents, Anthony and Geraldine, that he could not give evidence as he had to protect his girlfriend, child and family.

Judge Carroll Moran heard evidence that uncles of Liam Keane, Seanie and Kieran Keane, called to Roy Behan's home and offered him €30,000 as an inducement not to testify at the trial. Armed with a handgun, Kieran Keane warned Roy Behan if he made a statement, he would kill him and carry him away in the boot of a car. Judge Moran said there was evidence that Kieran Keane was a man who inspired fear and sentenced Roy Behan to a year in jail.

Afterwards, Anthony and Geraldine Leamy branded Roy Behan's sentence as disgraceful and said they felt let down by the judicial system, following the murder of their son.

'We go to his [Eric'] grave every day. He was a good kid, like. He worked in Tesco; he never missed a day in his life, never in trouble with the law. He was a great kid,' said Mrs Leamy, who wears a locket with a picture of her son.

Just a week after she ushered reporters away from her son, Liam, as they left the Central Criminal Court in Dublin, Margaret Keane, the wife of Christy, was at the centre of an abduction attempt. Around 2am on November 10, Margaret was brought to her home at Singland Gardens by taxi along with two friends, a husband and wife, having spent the night socialising in town. As the taxi pulled away, three men wearing balaclavas approached and surrounded her. A brief struggle ensued, but the mother's piercing screams could be heard by her two friends as the taxi was about to leave the area. The vehicle immediately returned, and the trio fled on foot, leaving Christy's wife relatively unharmed, but in a severe state of shock. The gang are thought to have jumped a wall at the rear of the Singland Gardens estate and made their getaway on nearby railway tracks. The men did not say anything to Mrs Keane during the course of the brief struggle, but it is believed that they intended to grab and gag her and, once this was done, telephone a fourth person waiting nearby in a getaway car. Gardaí suspected two of the men were also involved in the murder of Michael Campbell-McNamara less than two months previously. Following the attempted abduction, associates of Margaret Keane's jailed husband, Christy mounted a twenty-four-hour watch on the mother and the family home.

The collapse of the Eric Leamy murder trial and the conviction of the five men of the murder of Kieran Keane brought one of the worst years in terms of high-profile crime in Limerick to an end. Four lives had been directly claimed by the city's gangs in 2003. The exchanges between the opposing gangs were fuelled by a depth of hatred, which was, in truth, probably incomprehensible to an outsider.

In an interview with the *Sunday Independent* at the end

of 2003, city councillor and future Mayor of Limerick John Gilligan said there was no single or simple solution: 'There was a recent study which found that the most deprived place in Ireland was a small place on a mountain in Donegal, followed by Limerick City. There are areas of Limerick City which are the most socially disadvantaged in Europe. That hasn't happened overnight. It is the result of twenty years of government neglect.

'It took years for it to get this way and it will take years to put it right. There is a direct correlation between social deprivation and crime. If you keep telling people that they are outside the system and you keep shutting the door in their faces, what else do you expect? They become easy prey for those who are going to use them for their own nefarious ends.'

Sadly for Limerick, it would be another three years before the depth of the problem in the city's socially-deprived estates was acknowledged by government, at a national level, and a decision taken that a unique and radical approach was needed to address it.

8

Upping the Stakes

Attempts to broker a truce between Limerick's feuding factions were facilitated by local politicians in 2004. Events in late 2003 and early 2004 had confirmed fears that tensions were running high and the gangs were sourcing even more sophisticated and lethal weaponry.

Working on intelligence received, local gardaí, supported by members of the Emergency Response Unit (ERU), raided a rented house at Loughmore, Mungret, in June 2003. Gardaí uncovered a car bomb, Sterling sub-machine gun, 294 rounds of ammunition and a quantity of drugs. Four men were arrested and three were jailed when the case finally concluded in 2004.

In court, Detective Sergeant Tom O'Connor of Roxboro Garda station said the bomb was intended to 'put the feud on a more violent and bloody plain' and that 150 incidents had taken place in the ongoing criminal dispute. The deadly device would have been activated by a mercury-tilt switch when the vehicle moved. The crude metallic container was serrated to enhance the shrapnel effect. Gardaí suspected that the men were under instructions from the Keane gang who were within days, if not hours, of using the deadly device on a member of the Ryan gang.

Thirty-one-year-old Michael Scanlon, from St Mary's Terrace, Askeaton, County Limerick was sentenced to nine years' imprisonment after he pleaded guilty to possession of an explosive device, detonating chord, Sterling sub-machine gun and 294 rounds of ammunition.

Sean Smith, of the same age from Brixton, London, was sentenced to twelve years' imprisonment when evidence was proffered that the father-of-three was to be paid €10,000 to plant the bomb, which was intended to kill up to eight people. During Garda interviews, Smith said he would be paid after he planted the bomb and warned that he would be shot if he spoke to anyone about the matter.

Father of Sean, fifty-nine-year-old Richard Smith, also from London, was sentenced to five years' imprisonment after he allowed his rented home at Loughmore, Mungret, to be used to store the weaponry.

In January 2004, gardaí foiled another planned assassination by the McCarthy/Dundon gang when they raided a house in Moyross and recovered two sawn-off shotguns, two automatic handguns and a 1,000cc motorcycle. It was believed the motorcycle and weapons were to be used in an imminent hit.

In February 2004, gardaí in Limerick arrested one of Britain's most-wanted men and one of Limerick's most-feared men – Kenneth Dundon. The Southill man and father of Wayne, John, Dessie and Ger Dundon fled to Limerick after he brutally killed fifty-year-old Christopher Jacobs for having an affair with his wife, Anne McCarthy, in London. It later transpired in court that the relationship between Anne McCarthy and Jacobs, a heroin user, had begun after the pair met at a Department of Social Services office in August 2003, and she regularly spent nights at his flat in Hemsworth Court, Hobbs Place Estate, Hoxton.

On the night of October 8, 2003, having downed fifteen pints, Kenneth Dundon put on a mask, armed himself with a knife and kicked in the door to Christopher Jacobs' flat. The Limerick man stormed inside and started hitting Jacobs about the face and head. Anne McCarthy tried to intervene but was pushed out of the room. Kenneth Dundon stabbed Jacobs in the face and throat, leaving him to choke on his own blood. When Anne went back inside, she found Jacobs on the couch bleeding profusely from stab wounds to the face and neck. Blood covered his entire upper body. When the police arrived, they could do little to resuscitate the victim, and Christopher Jacobs suffocated to death.

Kenneth Dundon fled from the bloody scene and raced home to Pearson Street, Bethnal Green, east London, where he washed his clothes and shaved off his moustache. Police arrested him for the killing at the flat, at 3.55am.

In a police interview, Dundon claimed he went to Jacobs' flat looking for his wife with his sixteen-year-old son,

Gerard, but was told she was not there and spent the rest of the night at the pub. Dundon was released without charge on police bail, two days later, and fled to Limerick. By 2004, he had the dubious honour of being posted on Scotland Yard's most-wanted list and was arrested in Limerick under a European Arrest Warrant on February 11, 2004. However, he was not extradited back to Britain until September 2005, after making an unsuccessful appeal to fight the warrant to the Irish Supreme Court. He made Irish legal history when he became the first man to be arrested and extradited to another country under an EU warrant.

Because of eyewitness testimony to the killing, the prosecution accepted a guilty plea to a manslaughter charge, and Dundon was sentenced to six years' imprisonment. By the time he was sentenced, the killer had spent 951 days in custody, including 661 in Ireland waiting for extradition to Britain.

Hell hath no fury like a woman scorned, and the women caught up on either side of the Limerick feud were sometimes the driving force behind the tensions. On February 13, 2004, Limerick District Court heard evidence that five female relatives of Kieran Keane and Owen Treacy attacked women on the Ryan-side near the city centre in 2003. Owen Treacy's wife, Donna Treacy, St Munchin's Street, St Mary's Park, who was bound to the peace at the time of both offences, was given sentences totalling twelve months suspended on condition she keep the peace for two years. Donna's sisters-in-law, Norma and Aisling Treacy, Gillogue House, Clonlara, County Clare, and Anne Keane, Colmcille

Street, St Mary's Park and Donna Keane, Assumpta Park, Island Road, were each given three-month suspended sentences for their part in the incidents. All five women denied the charges.

The presiding judge said the women involved deserved to go to jail, because of the level of violence used, but said imprisoning them would only lead to 'difficulties' between the two sides, and none were locked up.

In another incident, on February 20, 2004, two nail bombs were thrown over the perimeter wall into Limerick Prison. One of the crude devices landed near the canteen area, while the other fell into the exercise-yard used by members of the Keane gang, but luckily both failed to explode.

That very evening, in a retaliation attack, a member of the McCarthy/Dundon/Ryan gang escaped with his life following a failed assassination attempt at the drive-through McDonald's restaurant in Dooradoyle. A pillion passenger on a motorbike opened fire on him, but, fortunately for the intended target, he was at the front of the queue and managed to speed away from the scene unharmed, as bullets flew into his car.

With twenty-five men jailed, or awaiting sentence, for their roles in the feud, public figures put themselves forward to act as brokers to bring an end to the violence. Junior Justice Minister, Willie O'Dea, conceded that the small criminal fraternity in Limerick were 'among the most violent, ruthless and brutal' you could find anywhere in the world. In the spring of 2004, representatives of the Collopy,

McCarthy/Dundon/Ryan gangs sent word to the politician that they wished to sit down and stop the spate of shootings amongst the rivals. A leading member of the Collopys, Brian Collopy (the man who murder victim Michael Campbell-McNamara tried to meet on the night of his killing) later told RTÉ's *Prime Time* of the hatred that existed between the St Mary's Park gangs and their opposition: 'It was kill on sight. If we got a phone call, we'd try to get one of them; if they got a phone call, they'd try to get one of us. It was blind madness. It was life or death. Them or us.'

In what was clearly one of the strangest gatherings ever held in the city, senior members of the three gangs travelled to Willie O'Dea's office for a preliminary meeting that March. Wayne Dundon arrived at O'Dea's office in a mini-bus, accompanied by four others.

'There was the Ryans; there was the Collopys and their people. We called to Willie O'Dea's office,' Wayne said.

A secret meeting to hammer out a peace deal was arranged for the same evening in a city hotel. Willie O'Dea alerted senior gardaí of the proposed meeting. Officers were extremely sceptical of any agreement among the city's criminals, given their experience in the past when a number of trials collapsed.

In a conference room booked by O'Dea's office, the Junior Justice Minister told some of the city's most-feared criminals that he had informed the gardaí the meeting was taking place and he would be reporting back to them after-wards. The Fianna Fáil TD sat alongside the then Mayor of Limerick, Dick Sadlier, at the head of the table, with members of the McCarthy/Dundons sitting alongside the Ryans on one side of the table. Sitting across from them were the Collopys.

However, the Keanes failed to attend. Brian Collopy had asked the Keanes to attend the meeting, but word was sent from prison that there was to be no member of the Keane gang at the conference.

Tentative agreements were reached between the Collopys and McCarthy/Dundons, and Wayne Dundon and Brian Collopy shook hands in front of O'Dea as the Collopys and McCarthy/Dundons agreed provisionally to halt attacks on each other.

Of the secret meeting, Willie O'Dea said on RTÉ's *Prime Time* that his focus was on the impact it could have on the wider community: 'My aim was to stop the violence. Of course I didn't feel 100 per cent comfortable about it [the meeting], but when I made my initial public comment about mediating, an awful lot of ordinary people came to me and said it would be a great idea if somebody could do something.'

While the various gang members considered the repercussions of the meeting with Willie O'Dea, one figure was to depart the scene. In June 2004, after two marriages and seven children, well-known criminal and former partner of murdered Eddie Ryan, Mikey Kelly, died after he suffered a gunshot wound to the head. His family maintained he was shot by a gunman, but investigating gardaí believed no other party was involved. Family members had Kelly's coffin later exhumed in a bid to prove no gun was hidden with his remains as was claimed in a newspaper report.

'Unhappy' was the mildest possible reaction that could be attributed to the Keanes when they learned that their associates, the Collopys, had made arrangements with their cross-city rivals, the McCarthy/Dundons. In July 2004, three members of the Collopy gang were double-crossed on a trip to Dublin to purchase a consignment of heroin worth €45,000. In Scribblestown Lane, they were met by members of Dublin's ruthless Westies gang who took the wads of notes from them at gunpoint and told them to 'fuck off back to Limerick' empty-handed. It was suspected that senior members of the Keane gang had formed an alliance with their Dublin counterparts and arranged the double-cross, to let their former associates know of their new set up.

A few weeks later, in what is understood to be a retaliation bid, gardaí intercepted two gunmen travelling to the home of Christy Keane, where they intended to carry out a drive-by shooting.

There is very little true loyalty, or friendship, in crime, and Limerick's gangs had fallen out in the past and major splits had occurred as was clearly evident with the deadly rift between Eddie Ryan and the Keanes. There were no major repercussions from the split between the Collopys and the Keanes, who soon returned to the business at hand, but it would not be the last time a criminal outfit in Limerick would suffer an internal schism.

As 2004 progressed, it was clear that some of the drug lords were determined to continue to wage war on their rivals and make the necessary preparations to do so. On

August 7, gardaí recovered a pipe bomb, two sawn-off shot-guns, some forty rounds of ammunition and a quantity of drugs buried in a yard at the rear of St Brendan's Street in St Mary's Park, stronghold of the Keanes. The bomb was made from a foot-long pipe, containing ball bearings and explosive powder.

Two months later, three quarters of a kilo of commercial explosives belonging to the McCarthy/Dundons, which gardaí say had the potential to do 'horrendous damage', was found hidden at the rear of a house in Ballinacurra Weston.

On December 13, a pipe bomb wrapped in plastic was uncovered in the attic of a shed at St Munchin's Road, St Mary's Park, after a shooting in the area earlier that day.

More and more explosives were been found by gardaí who suspected that dissident republican groups in the city were supplying the Keane gang with explosives and heavy-duty weaponry, including assault rifles, such as the AK-47 Kalashnikov. Dissident groups, however, refuted the claims, stating they had no involvement with organised criminal gangs. Despite the fact that senior members of both gangs had been killed or were serving lengthy sentences, the continuing discovery of explosives and firearms was further proof of the vicious level of intent that still remained in the feud.

Teenage son of Kieran Keane, Joseph, was targeted by a gunman in a botched hit on October 25, 2004. Two shots were discharged by a passenger on a motorcycle at the fifteen-year-old as he emerged from a fast-food takeaway in the Garryowen area, less than fifty metres from his home. One of the bullets lodged in a parked car outside the takeaway.

While there had been no feud-related murders since the death of Michael Campbell-McNamara a year previously, Chief Superintendent Gerry Kelly said gardaí were continuing to work on the premise that the feud was 'alive' and at no stage considered it to be dormant.

The senior Garda also admitted that his officers faced a very real threat in high-risk areas. A Garda patrol was shot at in Moyross the previous year and, following that, a decision was made to ensure that officers entering high-risk security areas did so with the assistance of heavily armed back-up. The armed detective unit from Cork was drafted in, to help their Limerick colleagues keep a lid on the city's criminals and the Garda chopper was put at their disposal. That October, a full-time Garda dog unit, which specialised in uncovering explosives and drugs, was assigned to the city.

In November 2004, Limerick State Solicitor Michael Murray warned that a mini-Mafia was developing in the city. The experienced solicitor said the latest upsurge in violent crime could not be dismissed as merely family feuds when, in reality, the city was facing an increasing level of organised crime.

'The authorities really haven't woken up to this, that there is this problem to be tackled. People who think this is not organised crime are living in cloud cuckoo land,' Mr Murray said.

The following month, fears that an innocent party would be the victim of the city's criminals was realised when a nineteen-year-old barman was shot after he refused Annabell Dundon, a sister of Wayne's, entry into a city pub. The episode which happened the week before Christmas shocked Limerick.

Ryan Lee was at the door of his uncle's pub, Brannigan's Bar on Mulgrave Street, on the night of December 19, 2004. The pub was particularly busy that Sunday night with many already in festive mood. Ryan was approached by Annabell Dundon at 9.30pm. She had been dropped off at the premises by her older brother, twenty-six-year-old Wayne. The young barman refused her admittance to the busy pub as she was underage. Wayne walked up to the door and remonstrated unsuccessfully with the barman on his sister's behalf. The well-known criminal then made the shape of a gun with his hand, pushed it against Mr Lee's face and said, 'F**k you, you're dead', and sat into a car and left.

Lee walked back inside the pub and began working behind the counter. Less than half an hour after Wayne Dundon made the threat, a man wearing a motorcycle helmet and carrying a handgun with a long barrel shot Lee twice. The first bullet hit him in the right hip and the gunman calmly turned to walk out the door, but then he turned back and callously discharged a second shot from close range into the left side of Lee's groin. The barman was left sprawling on the floor as customers hid in terror. The wounded barman's uncle, Stephen Collins, gave chase as the gunman walked from the pub and fled. Lee was rushed to the Mid-Western Regional Hospital and a massive Garda search in the city began.

Wayne Dundon was subsequently arrested and assaulted two detectives, Arthur Ryan and Brendan Casey, while being questioned in an interview room in Henry Street Garda station. Det Ryan's jaw was broken in the incident. The attack was captured on CCTV and Wayne Dundon spent Christmas and the New Year behind bars after his bail application was refused.

While waiting for his trial to be heard, he appeared in the Circuit Court the following April in a civil action case, seeking the return of a bulletproof vest which was seized by gardaí. Wayne Dundon denied that he was a member of any gang and told Judge Terence O'Sullivan that he wore the bulletproof vest as he had been shot at before. During the application, Wayne Dundon jumped from his seat and pulled down his pants exposing his bare buttocks to the judge. He bent over, slapped his bare buttocks and, pointing to them, said, 'See that your honour, that's what the Dundons think of you and the gardaí.'

The judge rose from the bench and received an apology from Wayne Dundon's defence counsel when the court resumed and decided to leave the matter rest.

In April 2005, Wayne Dundon pleaded not guilty to threatening to kill or cause serious harm to Ryan Lee and a jury was sworn in to try his case. However, Judge Carroll Moran had to discharge the jury after a son of one of the jurors was contacted by someone connected to the trial. The male juror said he had received two phone calls, one from his son and another from his son's girlfriend, saying they had been contacted by someone 'in the body of the courtroom', who informed them he had been selected for the jury. A new jury was sworn in and Wayne Dundon was found guilty of threatening to kill Lee.

After the trial, Wayne Dundon showed little interest in the court and tuned in to his earphones, rather than the legal proceedings, before he was sentenced. Addressing the judge, Detective Sergeant Eamon O'Neill of Henry Street Garda station said that, from his experience of working on investigations in Limerick, Wayne Dundon was one of the most violent criminals he has come across.

No one has ever been charged with the shooting of Ryan Lee, as the gunman wore a motorcycle helmet and could not be identified. After the young barman was shot, extensive damage was caused to Brannigan's pub when it was set alight in an arson attack. **GALWAY COUNTY LIBRARIES**

Judge Carroll Moran sentenced Wayne Dundon to ten years' imprisonment for threatening to kill Ryan Lee. Wayne Dundon also received two concurrent three-year sentences for assaulting the two gardaí in Henry Street. In February 2008, the Court of Criminal Appeal (CCA) reduced the ten-year sentence to seven years. The CCA was informed Wayne Dundon, who moved to Limerick from England when he was nineteen years old, intended to return to Britain upon his release. The CCA was satisfied that the ten-year sentence imposed on Wayne Dundon was 'unduly severe' and reduced the sentence by three years. Five months after the attack, Lee was still receiving medical treatment and counselling, but his family vowed not to be run out of Limerick by the series of events.

In their frantic bid to take control of Limerick's drug trade, the McCarthy/Dundons were the architects of their own demise. Wayne Dundon was, up until his conviction, one of the few leading members of the gang not behind bars after a plethora of high-profile and significant cases resulted in lengthy sentences for key figures in the gang. The list of gang members decommissioned by the relentless Garda crackdown over 2003 and 2004 was a family portrait of the McCarthy/Dundon gang. As meteoric as their rise to the top was, their descent was rapidly self-inflicted by their own crimes.

In 2005, all four of the Dundon brothers were behind bars. Twenty-two-year-old John Dundon, who was jailed for four and a half years for threatening to kill Owen Treacy during the Kieran Keane murder trial, had another sentence of twenty months' imprisonment imposed when he was convicted of threatening to burn down the home of a Limerick prison officer on August 21, 2001. His brother Dessie Dundon had already received a life sentence for Keane's murder, while eighteen-year-old Ger Dundon joined his older siblings behind bars in October 2005, after he committed three breaches of the public order act, thus breaking a bond to keep the peace, after he received a three years' suspended sentence for having €30,000 worth of ecstasy and cocaine when he was fifteen years old. Ger received the suspended sentence in April 2004 and was bound to the peace for three years, but within four months had committed the three public order offences.

While they were jailed, the gang was still able to orchestrate and conduct its affairs through a businessman, who gardaí believed to be the 'armchair general' for the entire operation.

Despite the jailings and convictions of all Dundon brothers, it was clear that the gang still cast a long and dark shadow over Limerick. On St Patrick's Day, 2005, eighteen-year-old Patrick Dowling from Deer Court, John Carew Park, Southill, was caught transporting a sub-machine gun in a taxi across the city. The high-powered M11 9mm Ingram sub-machine gun, which is capable of firing fourteen bullets within seconds, was collected near the University of Limerick and the young courier was moving it to John Carew Park when he was intercepted by gardaí in a taxi along Childers' Road. It was found in a white plastic bag along with 150 rounds of ammunition and a silencer.

When arrested Patrick Dowling, who suffered from ADHD and was living in a hostel for the homeless, said he did not know what he was carrying, but admitted to gardaí, 'I am f**ked now.'

Patrick Dowling pleaded guilty to possession of the firearm. At his trial in the Circuit Criminal Court, Detective Garda David Nolan of Roxboro Garda station told the court that the sub-machine gun was destined for the 'very sinister' McCarthy/Dundon gang. Det Nolan said it was significant that the defendant met a leading member of the McCarthy/Dundon gang in Limerick the day before being caught. It was accepted by officers that Patrick Dowling was not a member of the gang and he was sentenced to five years' imprisonment by Judge Carroll Moran in February 2006.

Investigations by the Criminal Assets Bureau (CAB) into the wealth of Limerick's gangs began at the turn of the Millennium. Indeed, Kieran Keane had been one of their prime targets, and officers were conducting a detailed examination of his affairs, before he was shot dead.

Some of the city's senior crime lords, who made millions of euro from drug-trafficking, also ran established businesses, before they first came to the attention of the authorities, making it harder to decipher what wealth they accrued from their legitimate businesses and what came from their illegal earnings.

In St Mary's Park it was estimated by gardaí that the Keanes owned at least thirty houses, which they purchased as a means to launder huge wads of cash. In some cases, if the gangs were not given first refusal to buy a house, the property would become the unfortunate scene of an arson attack.

One such person targeted by the CAB was Brian Collopy. In September 2005, the CAB sold his three-bedroomed home, Ashyby House in Fedamore, County Limerick, at a public auction for €225,000. The detached home was situated on three-quarters-of-an-acre site. The sale came about after CAB officers went to the High Court in November 2003 and were granted permission to freeze the legal holdings. The CAB was subsequently granted possession of the property in December 2004. Collopy had purchased the home in the 1990s for around £IRL60,000.

Mainly due to the efforts of gardaí in Limerick, there had not been a violent death in the division for almost fourteen months. However, this ended when twenty-five-year-old David 'Sid' Nunan from O'Malley Park, Southill, was released from prison on October 24, 2005, having served a two-year sentence for firearm offences. The young man had been before Limerick courts on numerous occasions and had racked up a long list of convictions. Within four days of his release, he was lured to a quiet village and shot dead. For all his errors, it seemed as if Nunan had a falling out with a Dublin criminal, while behind bars, and paid the ultimate price upon his release. It was suspected that Nunan's former associates, including members of the McCarthy/Dundon gang, facilitated the murder as a favour to the Dublin gang with whom they had established links. David 'Sid' Nunan was found with gunshot wounds to his back at the entrance to the courtyard of a private home in Parteen, County Clare, on October 28. While the victim's body was found in the neighbouring county, the murder had all the hallmarks of a Limerick gangland death. Nunan, who was staying in his sister's house, left the Southill home after dark to meet an associate, but instead walked into a murderous trap. It is believed he travelled by car across the city to the picturesque village of Parteen on false pretences, before he was lured down the laneway to the private home and shot in the back. His body was found by a passer-by. Despite the best efforts of investigating officers, nobody has ever been charged with Nunan's murder.

Just a week after Nunan's murder, Limerick was shocked at the death of an eighteen-year-old apprentice electrician, who was the victim of vicious assault by members from the Keane side of the feud.

Darren Coughlan of Pineview Gardens, Moyross, had never been in trouble before and was two years into his chosen trade. He was a dream son, had his whole life ahead of him and was the pride and joy of parents, Bernadette and Eugene. Darren was a first cousin of David 'Frog Eyes' Stanners, who was convicted of Kieran Keane's murder, but the trainee electrician had no involvement in any criminal activity. The apprentice electrician would often give neighbours or friends assistance.

The eighteen-year-old was out for the night with friends, walking along Old Cratloe Road near Limerick Institute of Technology, at 10pm on November 4, 2005, when a red Volkswagen Golf pulled up alongside him. Inside the car were three teenagers: Joseph Keane and his cousin, Richard Treacy, and friend, Shane Kelly.

All were on the Keane side of the feud. Joseph Keane, who lived with his mother, Sophie, at Greenhills Road, Garryowen, was the son of murdered Kieran Keane. Leaving Certificate student, Richard Treacy of St Munchin's Street, St Mary's Park, was the brother of Owen Treacy, who was abducted with Keane on the night he was murdered. Shane Kelly of Oliver Plunkett Street, St Mary's Park, was regarded as a very violent individual and had amassed seventy-one convictions by the summer of 2007.

On spotting Darren Coughlan, Kelly mistook the young

man for a member of the McCarthy/Dundon gang and jumped from the car with Treacy. Surrounded by his assailants, Coughlan tried to hold them off with a beer bottle before attempting to flee. As he ran off, he slipped on grass near the Limerick Institute of Technology and was beaten for about thirty seconds as he lay helpless on the ground. Coughlan suffered critical head injuries and was left in a semi-conscious state. He had the strength to phone his ten-year-old sister to ask for help, but his condition deteriorated dramatically after he was taken to the Mid-Western Regional Hospital and was immediately transferred to the intensive care unit, where he was placed on life support. At this stage, his attackers had already made their getaway from the scene in the car driven by Keane.

With his tearful family by his hospital bedside, Darren Coughlan died on Monday, November 7. Investigating gardaí soon brought those responsible to task. Treacy, Keane and Kelly pleaded guilty to Coughlan's manslaughter in June 2007.

Even innocent witnesses to serious events in Limerick could be targeted by criminals, and this became clear at the sentencing of the three before the Central Criminal Court (CCC) in 2007. The CCC heard that Darren's friend and a witness to the assault, Philip Healy, had lived with his family in a virtual prison since the violent death. They were under twenty-four-hour Garda protection, had security cameras installed around the home and steel shutters on their windows, to shield them from intimidation. Other family members and friends had been forced to move house because of their fear. Before the three were sen-tenced, Bernadette Coughlan told the Central Criminal Court that the death of her son would haunt her family for the rest of their lives. Keane's and Treacy's mothers both told the court their sons were remorseful. Sophie Keane pleaded for leniency and informed the judge she had already lost her husband and did not want to lose her son as well. However, Judge Carney rejected the notion that any of the guilty parties had shown any remorse and sentenced nineteen-year-old Keane and Treacy to six years in prison and twenty-year-old Kelly to seven years' imprisonment on July 30, 2007. As they were led away, the trio winked and smiled at their friends and supporters.

By mid-2005, in excess of fifty protagonists in the feud were behind bars, serving lengthy sentences for their involvement in the bitter gang-war, as well as serious organised criminal matters. However, the attacks continued as teenagers, anxious to impress their seniors, carried out the dirty work. Over the final two months of the year, gun crime in Limerick soared with an estimated fifty shooting incidents. Many of these incidents were related to a local-ised feud between two families in Moyross.

On November 29, 2005, an assassination attempt was made on Seanie Keane – brother of murdered Kieran Keane – at his home in St Mary's Park. Keane opened his front door to a caller at 7.30pm, and a gunman immediately opened fire, chasing Keane through the house and shooting at him four times, striking him twice in the arm and once in the lower back. The motive behind the attack is believed to have been personal and it was suspected that the Keane shooting was not feud related.

On December 22, an arson attack took place at Sophie Keane's home. A car stolen from the Raheen area of the city was rammed into the front gate and set alight, but the inferno was confined to the perimeter wall. This was the second time in the space of three months that the home, which is equipped with a CCTV system, had been targeted.

The outside world still did not realise how much the ravaged suburbs of Limerick had continued to deteriorate. Just how anarchic the situation had become was made all too clear shortly before Christmas.

The month before Garda officers had come under attack in Southill. An angry mob began throwing bottles and stones when gardaí stopped and questioned a gang leader in the suburb. A student garda was hospitalised after he was struck during the melee, and one man was arrested and convicted after the incident.

However, attitudes to the emergency services in the Limerick estates descended to an all-time low, three nights before Christmas, as gardaí and ambulance workers were jeered and jostled in O'Malley Park, while attempting to save the life of a teenage boy who lay unconscious on the footpath. Gardaí had come across the youth by chance and had contacted local ambulance services. While waiting for the ambulance, gardaí tried frantically to administer CPR themselves and were shouted and heckled by a growing number of youths. Officers received no co-operation from locals and had to determine for themselves that the youth's condition was brought about by substance abuse. Savage and venomous language was hurled at the gardaí as they desperately tried to revive the teenager. Nobody at the scene would inform gardaí what the boy had been doing, and when officers begged them to inform the ambulance workers what had happened, the mob stubbornly refused and showered the emergency services with further expletives. The ambulance crew tried to revive the boy on the way to hospital, but he was pronounced dead upon arrival.

For many law-abiding citizens in the city estates, life had become unbearable. The people of Southill, Moyross, St Mary's Park and Ballinacurra Weston felt abandoned, and an air of despair hung over these neighbourhoods. However, it would not be until September 2006, that the government finally sat up and really had to take notice.

9

The Hitman Confesses

A heavy-set, bald English man cut a lonely figure in his Port-laoise Prison cell, in May 2005. Inside his close confines, thirty-one-year-old James Martin Cahill was constantly reminded of his previous deeds and misdemeanours by a mind and conscience with little else to do apart from reflect upon his life to date. In March 2003, Cahill was caught in possession of an Uzi sub-machine gun and fifteen rounds of 9mm ammunition in Saggart, Dublin, and was subsequently convicted and jailed for five years. But it was his role in the murder of security manager Brian Fitzgerald, four months previous to the Dublin offence, which weighed heavily on his mind and he could no longer take the bitter isolation. The prisoner had begun to see a psychologist that year, because of the flashbacks of dark incidents he had been involved in. He confided to the psychologist that he often spoke to himself, but it was the murder which had completely eaten away at him and he asked prison officers if he could speak to gardaí.

Officers arrived and met with a highly apprehensive Cahill. Gardaí had already identified Cahill as the prime man, along with a number of associates, for the 2002 murder of Brian Fitzgerald, but the investigation was a long and protracted one and they needed a break to crack the case. Cahill was about to provide the State with their most important evidence yet.

'They are going to kill me,' Cahill said as he quietly confided to officers his role in the murder of Brian Fitzgerald. He was soon transferred to a more secure location and admitted that he had pulled the trigger and shot the father-of-two outside his home in November 2002, for €10,000. The contract killer told gardaí he couldn't sleep at night since the murder and wanted to get it out of his system and clear his conscience. Convinced that he was about to be murdered by those who, he alleged, ordered and assisted him in the horrendous deed, Cahill sang like a proverbial canary over the course of a number of detailed interviews up to November 2005 and named the other people alleged to have been involved.

The ongoing investigation intensified, and the following month, Cahill appeared before Limerick District Court, on June 15, and became the first person to be charged with Fitzgerald's murder. As was becoming common place for high-profile trials involving serious Limerick crimes, gardaí took no chances and officers with bulletproof vests patrolled the outside of the court. Inside the packed court room were Brian Fitzgerald's widow, Alice, and his parents, Martin and Bridie. Alice's eyes welled with tears as the defendant was led into court, and she momentarily lowered her head, before summoning the strength to face the man who had been charged with her husband's murder. The hearing lasted a minute and Judge Tom O'Donnell remanded Cahill in custody. Less than a fortnight after his initial court appearance, Cahill was sent forward to the Central Criminal Court for the murder trial and his case was heard before the year was out.

The investigation into Fitzgerald's murder was one of the biggest ever seen in Limerick, where major investigations were now occurring on a routine basis. In December 2002, the murder weapon – a CZ model 9mm pistol – was retrieved by Garda divers searching the bed of the Mulcair river, near Annacotty, on the city's outskirts. The discovery of the weapon opened a whole new investigation for the Limerick gardaí and their English counterparts.

Two shooting enthusiasts and members of Morecambe Rifle and Pistol Club in Lancashire, forty-nine-year-old Robert Naylor and fifty-six-year-old James Greenwood, were found guilty in 2004 of reactivating machine guns in a garden shed. After assembling the guns, they then sold the weapons on to the Limerick criminals through go-betweens. At the trial of the two men, the jury in the Old Bailey heard they were paid thousands of pounds (sterling) to restore Uzi 9mm, Sterling and Sten weapons to working order. Naylor and Greenwood travelled to arms fairs across the UK, looking for new models. Police said they turned to crime because of their fascination with firearms. However, it was the discovery of the self-loading 9mm pistol used in Fitzgerald's murder and the subsequent investigation which would lead to their downfall, after the gun was traced back to them in England.

An associate of Naylor's, James (Jimmy) Moloney, who lived in a caravan in Bradford, was put under surveillance after the discovery of the car bomb, Sterling sub-machine gun and drugs at the house in Mungret, in June 2003 (chapter eight). Fingerprints found on the bag containing the drugs belonged to a relative of Moloney and led to a surveillance operation being mounted in August 2003.

Jimmy Moloney, a father-of-seven, who regularly travelled to Ireland, was observed buying three guns from Robert Naylor for £4,000 in a Morecambe lay-by shortly after the surveillance operation began. Anti-terrorist officers swooped on Naylor and found the money under the seat of his car, while Moloney passed the weapons onto an associate, who was arming the McCarthy/Dundon gang in Limerick. He later told police, he intended selling the arms to 'people who may want to buy them', but had no one particular in mind. On November 19, 2004, Naylor and Greenwood were sentenced to ten years' and nine years' imprisonment, after they were convicted of manufacturing prohibited weapons and possessing firearms with intent to enable another to endanger life between the summers of 2002 and 2003. Forty-five-year-old Moloney, who pleaded guilty to firearms charges, was jailed for seven years for his role in the conspiracy to sell the firearms to the Irish gangs.

It was the 9mm semi-automatic pistol which had been reactivated in small shed in Lancashire by the two gun fanatics that had found its way into the hands of James Martin Cahill, via his connections in Limerick.

Cahill pleaded guilty to Fitzgerald's murder. When he took the stand before Mr Justice Paul Carney in November 2005, the murderer declared, 'I am willing to say that I will testify if a further case is coming.'

The Central Criminal Court heard that Cahill was one of two assailants who had gone to the Fitzgerald home at Brookhaven Walk, Corbally, in Limerick, on November 29, 2002 – Cahill's twenty-eight birthday. As the State hoped for further convictions, no identities, or the alleged circumstances leading up to the shooting, were made public until the trial of four men two years later.

The gunman, who was paid the €10,000 in two €5,000 instalments, was in complete fear of his life. Cahill asked that a transcript of the case be kept on file in case he was not around to provide future testimony. He was sentenced to life imprisonment on November 14, 2005.

As he was led to a waiting escort to begin his life sentence behind bars, Cahill told watching reporters, he believed his days in prison were numbered, 'I am going to be murdered in my cell tonight or in the next few days, watch.'

Having turned supergrass in one of the biggest criminal cases in the history of the State, Cahill was given round-the-clock protection and was kept in isolation from the rest of the prison population. At one stage, there were three prison officers with him at all times.

The same week as Cahill contemplated the rest of his life behind bars, former well-known barman, forty-one-year-old Jim 'Chaser' O'Brien, who fled from his Limerick home in 2003 after the Kieran Keane murder, was arrested on the continent as part of an operation by Belgian and Dutch police to smash a massive drug-trafficking network. Chaser O'Brien came from a highly regarded family, who ran a dairy farm in County Limerick, and was the last person who would have been considered to have associated with criminals. He was educated at the De La Salle Christian Brothers in Hospital, County Limerick, and entered the bar trade after leaving school.

Working in Limerick City watering holes, Chaser was considered to be an extremely competent barman who was well able to manage a busy pub. As he gained knowledge of the trade, he began his own business and purchased a bar in Pallasgreen on the main Limerick-Tipperary Road which he named 'Chaser O'Briens'. The pub and restaurant became extremely popular and was a frequent stop-off for motorists travelling in the east Limerick area. By the 1990s, O'Brien was now well acquainted with the pub trade and he bought the Henry Cecil pub and nightclub in Limerick City.

However, around the early to mid-1990s, Chaser's name began to pop up in Garda investigations into the drug trade in Limerick. In his private life, the 5ft 8ins, dark-skinned Chaser fancied himself as a lady's man and acted the part, wearing designer labels and driving a five-series BMW.

On May 3, 1998, twenty-year-old Georgina O'Donnell was shot dead in the Henry Cecil nightclub by twenty-nine-year-old Mark Cronin. Cronin, a father-of-three from Hyde Avenue, had a number of previous convictions for assault. He had had a series of arguments with his wife, Angela 'Biddy' Collins, and headbutted her in the Henry Cecil nightclub before leaving. He returned at 2am and was intent on shooting Angela, but accidentally shot his wife's friend, Georgina O'Donnell, through the eye instead. O'Donnell, the mother of a nine-month-old baby girl, collapsed on the dance floor and died the day after the shooting. Mark Cronin was subsequently convicted of the murder in the Central Criminal Court and sentenced to life imprisonment.

Subsequently, trade in Jim Chaser O'Brien's pubs declined and he left the business, but not before he had warranted further attention from the gardaí. In 2002, he was arrested in connection with an alleged scam involving stolen computer parts, but no charges were brought against him.

In the hours after the 2003 murder of Kieran Keane, Dessie Dundon was stopped driving O'Brien's Volvo car near Roscrea, County Tipperary, and falsely supplied Chaser's name to gardaí as he made his getaway from the region with Anthony 'Noddy' McCarthy. Although not involved in Keane's murder, Chaser was arrested afterwards, but was released without charge.

Tension had greatly increased in Limerick following Kieran Keane's murder. Chaser sought refuge in Spain but, having already established strong contacts with some of Europe's top drug dealers, he then relocated to Belgium before his arrest in 2005. In 2007, he was eventually sentenced to three years' imprisonment by Belgian authorities for charges relating to leading an international criminal gang. Chaser was also sentenced to five years' imprisonment for firearms and drug-trafficking offences.

As far as gardaí and prosecutors were concerned, the Brian Fitzgerald hit was ordered by a senior member of a Limerick gang whose dealers were refused entry to Doc's nightclub in Limerick City. Investigators wanted those responsible to be held accountable. Fitzgerald was identified as the single obstacle preventing the gang from selling their illegal wares inside the popular venue. In a sinister, prolonged campaign to intimidate and bully Fitzgerald, the gang fired a shot at his home in December 2001 and months later, his car was destroyed with paint.

Fitzgerald had had enough and reported the matter to gardaí who arrested a leading member of a crime gang. The young crime leader had a suspended sentence for violent disorder hanging over his head which would have been immediately reactivated if Fitzgerald testified against him in court.

Fearing for the safety of his family, Fitzgerald withdrew the complaint against the gang boss, but still afraid of further repercussions and the possibility of a future testimony against him, the gang member ordered that Fitzgerald should be taken out, and Cahill was contracted to assassinate the security boss.

Anthony Kelly of Cragg House, Kilrush, County Clare, a man with a chequered past, was also questioned about the murder plot. A fair-haired man, Kelly was well known throughout Clare and oversaw a warehouse and furniture business and had assets in China and mainland Europe. The investigation into the murder of Brian Fitzgerald was not Kelly's first brush with the law. Over a twenty-four-year--period, he earned six convictions, including two for larceny, on one occasion for IR£30,000-worth of stolen bicycles. In February 1984, twenty-six-year old Kelly was convicted for living off the immoral earnings of prostitution. He had provided prostitutes to farmers in west Clare directly to their isolated homes or in his 'passion wagon'. Kelly received a nine months' prison sentence for the offence.

In Kilrush, he ran a thriving warehouse business where he bought and sold a vast array of goods from golf clubs to children's prams. He played rugby for his home town and served as team captain. In 1997, after an investigation by the Criminal Assets Bureau into his earnings, he settled with the agency for a six-figure sum.

In August 2003, Kelly survived an assassination attempt when seasoned Limerick criminal John Creamer shot him four times at his home. Kelly was making a cup of tea in his kitchen when the would-be assassin fired eight shots at him through the window. Kelly survived the hit as his double-glazed windows decreased the velocity of the bullets. While recovering, armed gardaí stayed with Kelly in the Mid-Western Regional Hospital.

Less than a year after James Martin Cahill was sentenced to life imprisonment, forty-nine-year-old Anthony Kelly was arrested in May 2006 in connection with the Fitzgerald murder and was questioned and later released. After journeying to Morocco and Britain, he was arrested again on October 16, on his return to Ireland. He was in Limerick District Court the following day and was charged with Fitzgerald's murder. Before the same court a week later, his defence solicitor Eugene O'Kelly said the accused man would be pleading not guilty to the charge as there was 'no basis for the allegations'.

As is the law, anyone who is charged with murder and wishes to make a bail application must apply to the High Court and Anthony Kelly did so a fortnight after he was arrested. At the High Court sitting in Cloverhill, in Dublin, the defendant offered to have his sister pay an independent surety of €75,000 to guarantee his release, but Detective Sergeant Seamus Nolan of Mayorstone Garda station, who was investigating the case, said he would not be satisfied with 'a surety of €75 million'. Judge Paul Butler refused the bail application.

Cahill had also identified a young Limerick man as his accomplice in Fitzgerald's murder. In May 2005, this man had been sentenced to two years' imprisonment when he threatened to have a Limerick prison officer 'blown away' for €20,000. The Limerick criminal had bragged to the officer that he had shot people in the city for €10,000 and would have no difficulty spending twice that figure to have the officer killed. Only aged twenty-one at the time, the young man told the officer that he would get him and his family, if it was the last thing he did. The prison officer was also warned by the twenty-one-year-old that he still had to go out the Dublin Road each evening. The sinister threat was made as prison officers attempted to restrain the Limerick man while on remand at the prison on May 26, 2004. Passing sentence, Judge Carroll Moran noted that the man was known as a very violent individual and that the courts are expected to protect prison officers.

On December 5, 2006, senior gardaí had the young Limerick man along with Anthony Kelly and brothers, twenty-six-year-old John Dundon and twenty-two-year-old Dessie Dundon of Hyde Road, Ballinacurra Weston, brought to Limerick courthouse under tight security, and the four men were sent forward to the Central Criminal Court for trial.

When the four were charged with Brian Fitzgerald's murder, Dessie Dundon was already serving a life sentence for Kieran Keane's murder, while John Dundon was locked up for threatening to kill or cause serious harm to Owen Treacy during the Keane murder trial. The other young Limerick man was already in custody, having been charged with the 2006 murder of 'Fat Frankie' Ryan.

The trial of the four men charged with Fitzgerald's murder finally began on October 16, 2007 – almost five years since his death. All four pleaded not guilty to the charges. Dublin's Cloverhill courthouse was chosen as the venue for the trial and a mammoth security operation was put in place for the duration of the high-profile case. An all-male jury was sworn in and, conscious of the massive media interest in the case, Mr Justice Peter Charlton issued a blanket ban on the jury from reading any media reports on the trial until it had concluded. The twelve jurors were also told they would be excused from jury service for the rest of their lives when they had reached their verdicts. It was clear from the very beginning this was going to be a highly emotionally-charged case.

Neighbours of the Fitzgerald family provided evidence:

A woman recalled that she was woken at 3.37am by someone shouting, 'Oh God, no!' She then heard two or three shots and another volley thirty seconds later.

Another female neighbour said she heard four or six shots and a man calling out, 'Help me, I'm being shot at.'

Other residents recalled seeing men wearing light-coloured motorcycle helmets and dark clothing in the estate. Taxi drivers gave evidence of seeing a motorcycle with two passengers on board speeding through Corbally and the same motorbike on fire in a laneway at Dillons' petrol station on the Dublin Road.

CCTV evidence was provided of the young Limerick man walking in Pineview Gardens, Moyross, hours before the murder, and a clip was shown of a man wearing similar clothing and driving a motorcycle, at 1.20am, in the northside city estate, just hours before the murder across the city.

Two weeks after the case began, the State's main witness James Martin Cahill sat in the witness box, to give his version of events leading to up the murder, the shooting and the aftermath. His evidence was crucial and had to be watertight for the prosecution.

Cahill was born and lived in Birmingham, but moved to the west coast of Clare to live with an uncle when he was fifteen years old. There he met Anthony Kelly through a friendship with Kelly's two sons.

Legal constraints meant that some of those whom Cahill implicated in the murder could not be identified as they were not before the court. Cahill alleged that a man, categorised to the court as Mr A, ordered the hit on Fitzgerald as the nightclub security manager had made a statement to gardaí against him. Cahill testified that he agreed to carry out the murder for a sum of €10,000. In late November, 2002, he had a series of meetings with Mr A and also met a Mr C, who said he would drive a motorbike when asked by Mr A to do a job. Cahill said he met Mr B in a restaurant in Portlaoise and Mr B then brought him to Anthony Kelly's house in Clare. Cahill alleged that Kelly provided him with the gun and showed him how to use it. Shortly before the murder, Cahill claims he and Mr B met the two Dundon brothers and later met Mr C, who drove from Dublin, but was having clutch problems with his Ducatti motorbike.

They returned to Mr B's home, and Mr C became uneasy about his role in the murder and said he wanted to pull out. The young Limerick man was selected to fill the void and agreed to drive a motorbike to Fitzgerald's home.

Prior to the murder, Cahill claimed that he had been shown Brian Fitzgerald's home by the Dundon brothers and scouted the neighbourhood for a good place to hide until Fitzgerald arrived home from work. He told the court that he was then driven to Doc's nightclub, where he claimed Dessie Dundon pointed out Fitzgerald to him. Cahill admitted to walking straight past the man he was about to murder, before he returned to the Brookhaven Walk estate with his accomplice. The pair hid in bushes, until they received a call saying Fitzgerald was on the way home. At 3.15am, Fitzgerald left the nightclub.

On his return home Fitzgerald parked his jeep in the driveway and opened the door to step out. Cahill decided this was his opportunity. Wearing a motorcycle helmet, he ran up to the father as he got out of the vehicle. There was a struggle and Cahill fired four shots, hitting Fitzgerald once. Using his incredible physique, the wounded man managed to find his feet and ran up the streets, shouting for help. Cahill gave chase. In the commotion, Cahill twisted his ankle, and a frantic Fitzgerald started banging on a neighbour's door, but the gunman caught up with him and shot him across the bonnet of a car. Fitzgerald fell to the ground and Cahill walked around his body, pointed the handgun and shot the Limerickman in the head.

Cahill and his accomplice fled from the area on the motorbike and Cahill gave the Limerick man his helmet to burn with the motorbike and then made off in a red Ford Mondeo, while his accomplice got a taxi back out to Moyross. Cahill returned to Mr B's house, dumped the gun in a hedge and got changed out of the clothes he had worn for the murder. He travelled to Dublin and met up with Mr A. From there they moved on to Belfast, where they stayed for a few days, before journeying on to England. Cahill then claimed to have met Anthony Kelly in a Manchester hotel.

The cross-examination of Cahill by the defence barristers of the four accused turned out to be decisive. The Englishman came under intense scrutiny. Within days, gaping holes started to appear regarding Cahill's testimony against Anthony Kelly and the Dundon brothers.

Cahill said he heard screaming and voices in his head, which only went away when he began to confess to the crimes he had committed. The court heard that the murderer wanted to get the evidence right, but had got jumbled up with another violent death that had been planned. He openly contradicted himself when, in cross-examination, he said he walked past Fitzgerald with the two Dundon brothers outside Doc's nightclub on November 26, two days before the date he had previously stated.

Doubts about the time the gun collection was arranged were proffered, along with the length of various journey times from different accounts of Cahill's evidence. He also said John Dundon was not present when Brian Fitzgerald was identified to him, or when the Corbally home was pointed out to him. Cahill said while John Dundon was in the house where the murder was discussed, he was not present for the conversation itself. At one stage Cahill spoke of further voices and said he 'didn't want to convict someone in the wrong'. Furthermore his evidence against Anthony Kelly and Dessie Dundon was not corroborated as the judge pointed out to the jury.

The State's case against all but the young Limerick man had begun to tear at the seams. Cahill had contradicted earlier testimony and statements he provided to gardaí, and proved to be an unreliable witness. Defending Anthony Kelly, Michael O'Higgins SC said Cahill's sister and brother had told gardaí he was a compulsive liar. A statement from Cahill's sister read to the jury claimed he lied, stole from and betrayed every member of his family. Cahill admitted he hoped for a new life abroad under the witness protection programme.

On November 8, the prosecution case wound up and, the following day, Mr Justice Peter Charlton directed the jury to acquit John Dundon as there was no case against him. All charges against John Dundon were immediately dropped and he was cleared of any involvement in the murder case.

The jury began their deliberations on November 14 and, the following day, after five hours, acquitted both Anthony Kelly and Dessie Dundon of the murder, but found Cahill's accomplice guilty of the offence, earning him a life sentence. Already convicted for the murder of Kieran Keane, Dessie Dundon returned to prison, while Anthony Kelly walked free from Cloverhill courthouse that evening, grinning at the cameras in the company of his then partner, Marie Cronin. Defence solicitor, Eugene O'Kelly said he was grateful to the jury for upholding Anthony Kelly's innocence, but expressed his resentment for his client's incarceration for a year 'on the word of a self-professed perjuring, perverted killer'.

Mr O'Kelly told the media throng, 'It is quite extraordinary that this man's freedom has been denied to him for the past year on the rantings and the ravings of a demented psychopath.'

Just as Anthony Kelly was found not guilty and returned home to Kilrush that evening, a free and innocent man, other members of his family were about to be locked up for gun crimes. His son twenty-year-old Richard and nephew twenty-six-year-old James Kelly pleaded guilty at Ennis Circuit Court to firearm charges. They were both convicted of possession of stolen, sawn-off shotguns in the grounds of Anthony Kelly's home in Kilrush. Anthony Kelly had been locked up at the time, but his son had access to the west Clare house.

A media ban on reporting the son and nephew's case had been imposed until the completion of the Fitzgerald trial. The pair was recorded moving shotguns from one part of the property to shrubbery outside, on video evidence secretly set up by gardaí to provide surveillance. In April 2007 they were arrested as they went to collect the weapons and, initially, they denied knowledge of them, but admitted responsibility when the video evidence was shown to them. The shotguns had been stolen and modified and Richard was sentenced to five years' imprisonment, while James was jailed for four years.

At the time of the murder trial in 2007, two other men from Limerick, who were involved in the network of Brian Fitzgerald's death, were jailed in Britain and on the continent for serious offences. It seems highly unlikely they will ever be tried for Brian Fitzgerald's chilling murder.

10

Moyross Arson Attack

A report published in a travel guide in the 1990s, which contended that Limerick was best viewed through a rear-view mirror, has long being held in contempt by its people, civic leaders and tourist chiefs across the Mid-West.

However, by 2006, renowned tourist bible, the Lonely Planet, gave the city a much needed boost when it described Limerick as a cosmopolitan enclave with a warm heart. According to Lonely Planet, Limerick's well-known reputation was one that wasn't deserved: 'Limerick City continues to develop into a busy shopping centre full of upbeat restaurants and buzzing bars, and with a storming club and entertainment scene.'

But, as noted by the travel guide, the city would continually be judged by the occurrence of crime. In this respect, serious offences committed in Limerick were considerably lower than in other Garda divisions across the country. Just one murder was recorded in Limerick in 2005 (the murder of David Nunan in Parteen, County Clare, could also be deemed a Limerick murder in all but location), but the official figures still showed far fewer killings than in Dublin, Waterford, Kerry, Clare, Westmeath, Wexford, Wicklow, Cork or Galway. Four violent deaths were recorded in Limerick in 2004, nine in the previous year and more than 90 per cent of the 47 cases of violent death in Limerick since 1997 have been solved by gardaí, a success rate described as 'incredible' by former Limerick Chief Supt Gerry Kelly.

However, there was also a sharp increase in shooting incidents in the latter half of 2005. In 2005, of the 313 shooting incidents recorded in the State, Limerick accounted for 83 incidents of illegal discharge of firearms.

From court cases heard at the beginning of 2006, it became evident that the different criminal gangs instilled and maintained extensive fear across their strongholds, and no amount of Garda work or condemnatory speeches from politicians and local councillors could loosen the vice-like grip which they held over vulnerable parts of their communities.

A Limerick priest informed the Central Criminal Court in Dublin how he was told to pass on a death threat to a fifty-nine-year old man, who was facing sentencing for possession of €21,000 worth of cannabis. The drugs mule had picked up the drugs in Ballymun and had been directed to leave the cannabis in a wheelie bin at the Parkway Shopping Centre. The priest recalled how he was directed to tell the guilty man not to give gardaí any names.

'That's a confessional father,' said the gang member who issued the warning.

No names were provided to gardaí and the drug runner was jailed for two years.

Shootings continued in Moyross and St Mary's Park in separate incidents, in February and March 2006. On March 3, gardaí preserving the scene of the city's latest 'tit-for-tat' shooting incident in St Mary's Park came under fire from a passing gunman at 4.30am. Two houses had been shot at in St Munchin's Street and the Garda members were in their patrol car at the scene when five gunshots were fired at their car. Two days later, a man, aged in his early twenties, was shot in the foot, in Craeval Park, Moyross.

It was clear to all, amid the horror of the crimes committed, that criminal access to deadly firearms was a major problem. Of the seventeen recorded shooting incidents in the Southern Garda Region, which took in divisions in Cork, Kerry and Limerick for the first few months of 2006, fifteen of them occurred in Limerick.

At a Teachers' Union of Ireland congress in mid-April, a teacher spoke of her experiences in a Limerick school which she described as 'absolute hell on earth'. She went on, 'Where I teach, I meet students every day who have come from housing estates, where there would have been drive-by shootings the previous night. And they talk casually about going and bringing out their sawn-off shotguns. That sort of talk obviously makes teachers very nervous.' The speech received a standing ovation from the floor.

2006 was only to get worse, and for one Southill family their lives would be affected forever by an, as yet, unsolved murder.

Seventeen-year-old Richard 'Happy' Kelly came from O'Malley Park and was diagnosed with ADHD at the age of ten while in primary school. However, he also had a reputation with gardaí and the city's juvenile courts. He had numerous convictions for car thefts.

Unfortunately for 'Happy', on the night of April 23, it appears he set out to steal the wrong car. As thousands made their way back to Limerick, having witnessed Munster trounce Leinster in the Heineken Cup semi-final, 'Happy' waved goodbye to his mother, Mary, as he left their family home. Weeks beforehand, he had learned he was the father of a baby boy and was said to be delighted. As 'Happy' walked away into the O'Malley Park estate on that Sunday night, his mother did not realise it would be the last time she would see her youngest son. He was spotted later that night at Daly's Cross near Castleconnell on the Dublin Road, at 2.30am, but was never seen again.

Within days, gardaí at Roxboro began searches alongside the busy N7 approach route to the city. Days passed without a trace of 'Happy' and officers classified him a category 'A' missing person.

His mother, Mary, made numerous emotional appeals for information on her son's whereabouts, but weeks became months and still there was no trace of him. It was openly accepted that the only solace that could be provided to the Kelly family now was the discovery of a body, to allow the heartbroken mother bury her son.

The mystery of the missing seventeen-year-old took a sinister turn in late November 2007, when fishermen tending to their lines in Lough Bridget, east Clare, snagged and pulled skeletal remains from the lake. The Killaloe gardaí were informed of the grim discovery. The Garda underwater unit collected more remains from the bottom of the lake, including ropes and concrete blocks, of the type that would be used to secure railings at construction sites. The remains were sent to Dublin for forensic examination and, on December 7, 2007, following extensive DNA testing, gardaí confirmed the body was that of 'Happy' Kelly. Nineteen months after he disappeared, a full murder investigation was launched.

The exact circumstances surrounding 'Happy's' killing still remain a mystery. The most accepted theory is that the teenager's bad habits led him into an episode of fatal misadventure. It is believed that 'Happy' stole a car belonging to a Limerick City drugs gang, which, unknown to him, contained a hidden cache of drugs, firearms or cash. 'Happy' is believed to have burnt the car out before the criminal outfit caught up with him. He was then cruelly killed and his body dumped in the east-Clare lake. To date, no-one has been charged with 'Happy's' murder.

A fortnight after the disappearance of Kelly, the shootings continued. On May 8, 2006, at 5am, a forty-two-year-old man suffered a non-fatal gunshot wound to the thigh in Oliver Plunkett Street, St Mary's Park. Two days later, as two criminals and members of the McCarthy/ Dundon gang got into their car in Moyross, a hail of bullets was fired at them. They managed to flee from the area, but worse was to follow hours later.

Nineteen-year-old Aidan Kelly from College Avenue, Moyross, and his girlfriend were expecting the birth of their first child in the summer of 2006. Aidan had successfully applied to Limerick City Council for social housing at Cliona Park near his family home. He was the second youngest of a family of five and the son of taxi driver Liam and his wife, Mary, who had four other sons and one daughter. Aidan had previous offences for car theft and other road-traffic offences. He was on bail for a number of robberies of homes in east Clare and was considered by gardaí to be linked to individuals on both sides of the city's feud. However, this treacherous tightrope that Kelly attempted to negotiate was too fraught and cost him the ultimate price. Aidan never got to see his baby.

On the night of May 10, Kelly was lured to his death in a quiet laneway in Blackwater, County Clare. His silver Opel Astra was found abandoned at the entrance to the area. His body was discovered six yards away with a rifle underneath it. He had been shot up to five times, at least once through the head, in the upper torso and in a leg. His mobile phone was also recovered at the scene, and it was initially hoped that this would provide detectives with vital clues as to who the culprits were.

Speaking outside the family home, Liam Kelly said his family was 'devastated' about the murder of his son. 'You wouldn't believe it,' the grieving father said.

There was no sign of a let-up in gun-related crime in the usual spots across the city. For the majority of Limerick people, this violence was only an issue brought into their world when reported by the media. However, families continued to flee their homes in Southill and Weston throughout the year as the shootings and intimidation continued.

On May 20, Munster won the Heineken Cup, and the city celebrated for days on end. The images of Limerick's main thoroughfare packed with thousands of supporters cheering on their team in Cardiff and broadcast across the world was one of the best unintended publicity coups ever achieved. Yet in the deprived estates, the contrast could not have been starker – life continued the same, success or no success.

The summer arrived and, on June 14, gardaí prevented further violence in the city and a possible attack on a senior gang member when they swooped on an Egyptian national, thirty-six-year-old Ibrihme Hassan and a Dublin man on the city's southside and recovered a loaded pistol with silencer attached. In court, the following year, Hassan, a chronic heroin user, said he was ordered by the country's most dangerous criminals to collect the gun from a Limerick gang and deliver it to Dublin, to repay a heroin debt.

Hassan, with an address at Priory Lodge, Celbridge, County Kildare, changed his not guilty plea, on the second day of the trial, and was re-arraigned before Judge Carroll Moran. He is originally from Cairo, but moved to Ireland in 1991 and married a Dublin woman. At the time of his plea, they had one daughter aged five, and Hassan previously worked as a chef, but started using heroin following a road-traffic accident. Hassan told gardaí during questioning that he was ordered to collect the weapon in Limerick by a major Dublin drug dealer, who he owed over €1,000 for heroin. The Egyptian said he was under pressure to pay the debt and met an eighteen-year-old man in Limerick, who supplied him with the gun at Prospect Hill.

Detective Sergeants Eamon O'Neill and Kevin McHugh were on patrol on the city's southside, on June 14, when they noticed two vehicles parked near each other. The officers observed Hassan take a package from his jacket and put it into the glove compartment of a silver Ford Galaxy car. Hassan, with another man, then got into a waiting, black Volkswagen Golf and drove off, but they were stopped and arrested at the junction of Edward Street and Wolfe Tone Street. The alert officers recovered the fully loaded Sphinx semi-automatic pistol, with a silencer attached, and six rounds of .38mm ammunition in the Ford Galaxy. The safety on the weapon had been turned off and there was one round in the breach; the gun was cocked and ready for immediate use.

In Limerick Circuit Criminal Court, Det Sgt O'Neill said Hassan 'was dealing with some of the most serious criminals in the country'.

Before passing sentence, Judge Carroll Moran said he had to take into account aggravating and mitigating factors.

'The gun was in a dangerous state and in a condition ready to fire. There was a silencer attached and when fired, it would have been difficult, if not impossible, to know where the shot came from ... The transport of dangerous guns is a serious offence. It can be considered more serious than the transport of large quantities of illegal drugs ... The Oireachtas has given strong messages that possession of drugs is to be treated harshly,' commented Judge Moran.

The judge imposed two three-year sentences for the separate offences, to run alongside each other; possession of the loaded gun with intent to endanger life and possession of ammunition with intent to endanger life. Scepticism prevailed amongst gardaí in Limerick as to the explanation given by Hassan for committing the offence, and it is widely believed the weapon was to be used for a deadly purpose against a well-known gang member.

Shortly after Hassan's arrest, twenty-eight-year-old Larry McCarthy Junior, of no fixed abode but with addresses at Hyde Road and the Old Cork Road, Southill, and a cousin of Wayne, John, Dessie and Ger Dundon, was jailed for eleven years in England for being a 'sales rep' for an arms supermarket. Larry McCarthy Junior was found guilty of being the 'middleman', for bringing customers to a couple who turned their one-bedroom flat in Hackney, east London, into an 'ammunition depot', stocked with a machine gun and hundreds of live rounds. Larry McCarthy Junior was found guilty of conspiracy to possess a firearm with intent to endanger life and conspiracy to possess a prohibited weapon in July 2005. He had denied both charges at Southwark Crown Court. When police raided the tiny flat, the previous year, they found a Mach II sub-machine pistol and fifty varieties of ammunition, including 700 live rounds and 500 bullets in various stages of production.

Back in Limerick, surveillance on the city's criminals continued. In 2005, Justice Minister Michael McDowell announced the gardaí were to receive €6.5m to fund 'Operation Anvil', to tackle organised crime, primarily in Dublin. The security initiative utilised a combination of intelligence-driven and high-profile policing. It was extended nationwide in 2006 and had its first success outside of the capital with one of the biggest hauls of weapons, ammunitions and drugs detected in Limerick.

The National Surveillance Unit gathered information on specific targets. On June 29, following an intensive two months of close monitoring of the city's gangs, more than fifty members of the gardaí swooped on several locations across the city.

The haul recovered was unprecedented. Along with almost a thousand rounds of ammunition, seven high-powered firearms (two machine pistols and five handguns), six stun guns, drugs paraphernalia, heroin and cocaine, worth in excess of €1m, were recovered.

A former underage rugby coach, thirty-five-year-old Aidan Radmall from Corbally, was arrested at his flat. He worked as a barman and bouncer in the city and had never been in trouble before.

The following day, in further searches, three rifles and a box of ammunition were found at the back of a house in St Mary's Park.

Radmall was held in custody and admitted to gardaí that

he acted as a runner for a city criminal gang and made a number of trips abroad, to assist in their international underworld operation, and was involved in the storage and distribution of weapons and drugs. He made four trips to the Netherlands for the gang, after accruing a debt. In a bid to distance himself from the gang, he moved to Clare but allowed his apartment in Cecil Street to be used as a safe house. He pleaded guilty to having heroin worth €400,000, amphetamines with an estimated street value of €38,000 and cannabis worth €100 for sale or supply in a city-centre flat. He also pleaded guilty to the unlawful possession of a Glock semi-automatic pistol, an Intra Tech sub-machine gun, a Skorpian machine pistol, a Beretta semi-automatic pistol, six stun guns and almost 1,200 rounds of ammunition. He was sentenced to seven years' imprisonment, which was later appealed to the Court of Criminal Appeal by the DPP for being unduly lenient, but the sentence was upheld.

The arrest of Hassan with the loaded pistol and silencer, the jailing of Larry McCarthy Junior and the uncovering of the massive cache of arms and drugs formed a backdrop to a summer of violence in Limerick.

At 4.15am, on June 19, at Cornmarket Row in the city centre, a training grenade was thrown through the ground-floor window of the apartment of a grandmother of the McCarthy/Dundons. The first officers to arrive at the scene did not know whether the grenade was real or not, and nearby homes were evacuated until the Defence Forces Explosive Ordinance Disposal (EOD) team from Cork ensured there was no threat.

On July 8, a family home was shot at in Sunnyside Court, Carew Park, Southill. Two days later, a lone gunman fired at a car parked in Oliver Plunkett Street, St Mary's Park, while in another incident, the car belonging to Sophie Keane, widow of murdered Kieran Keane, was targeted by gunmen outside her Garryowen home.

Gun crime across the city was widespread on the night of July 20. It began at 10pm when a sixteen-year-old youth was shot in the leg during a drive-by shooting in O'Malley Park, Southill. The teenager, a distant relation of John Dundon through marriage, was not the intended target, as the gunman armed with a semi-automatic handgun was aiming at a man in his thirties, who associated himself with the McCarthy/Dundon gang. The car used in the shooting was later found burnt-out in Annacotty. Five hours later, at 3am, the home of 'Fat' John McCarthy in Cliona Park, Moyross, was also fired on. McCarthy was the nephew of murdered brothers Eddie and John Ryan, and his home had been previously targeted in an AK-47 attack, in 2002. Minutes later, gunmen opened fire on the home of Eddie Ryan's widow, Mary, in Kileely, and an upstairs window was shot through. At the same time, a resident in Caherdavin Heights discovered a 'grenade-like' device placed in their sitting room and gardaí again contacted the EOD team, who carried out a controlled explosion in nearby woods.

An idea of just how bad the situation had become was recorded over five successive violent nights in Limerick. On July 23, two separate shooting incidents in Ballinacurra

Weston were recorded. In the early hours of July 24, the grandmother of the McCarthy/Dundon family members was targeted again, but in a far more sinister fashion when a gunshot was fired at her home while she slept inside. Shots were also fired in Crecora Avenue, Ballinacurra Weston, and a sawn-off shotgun recovered in St Mary's Park. Two homes of female partners of McCarthy/Dundon gang members were targeted by arsonists. Armed gardaí were patrolling the strongholds of the gangs, but the violence continued. In the early hours of July 27, gardaí received reports of shots fired at three homes in Kilalee, John Carew Park and St Mary's Park. Five families fled their homes the same week, following arson attacks and further intimidation. Within seven days, eleven shooting incidents had been recorded across the city and everyone waited with baited breath as to what would happen next.

The violent exchanges looked set to become far worse and it soon became clear that all people, including children, were viewed as legitimate targets. After a lull that existed for just over a fortnight, two children aged eight and twelve years old narrowly avoided serious injury when a gunman opened fire in a drive-by shooting in Garryowen, at 9.10pm on August 14. Junior members of Geraldine's soccer club had been training on a green area just before the shooting. The car understood to be used was stolen the night before and was later found burnt-out in Ballyclough on the outskirts of the city. As with many other shooting incidents which would occur in the city in the latter half of the year, no official complaint was made to gardaí.

On August 23, the feud was propelled into the leafy Kilteragh estate in Dooradoyle. Drug dealer, thirty-year-old John McNamara miraculously escaped with his life when twenty bullets tore through his car and the façade of his girlfriend's home. McNamara raced for cover and managed to dodge the hail of fire. An associate of Philip Collopy, he had already received serious facial injuries and lost an eye as the result of a shooting incident in 2000 in O'Malley Park, Southill. He had also been stabbed with a pitchfork in another attack by a leading member of the McCarthy/Dundon gang. McNamara, who had convictions for drug dealing and firearm offences, had been arrested earlier in the summer as part of 'Operation Anvil'.

After the attack on August 23, Supt Frank O'Brien said, 'It was a completely reckless act in a residential area which absolutely defies belief.'

Five days later, gardaí received a report that an associate of John McNamara's had been walking through Dooradoyle, during evening rush-hour traffic, when he was targeted by a gunman on a motorbike. The following day, on August 29, gardaí had to respond to another night of feud violence when a home in Richmond Park, Corbally, was petrol-bombed, while Garryowen and Moyross were the scenes of further gunfire. Come August 30, Judge Leo Malone had to flee from the district courtroom after a fracas, involving more than thirty people on either side of the feud, erupted outside the court and spilled into the main courtroom. Six people were arrested following the riot and charged with public-order offences.

In the midst of gang's attempts to wipe each other out, the city's youth were left to their own devices in learning how to handle firearms. On August 28, in Crecora Avenue, Ballinacurra Weston, a sixteen-year-old girl had to be hospitalised when she received a ricochet from a gunshot. A group of teenagers had been engaged in late-night target practice. A fortnight later, outside his St Ita's Street home in St Mary's Park, a fifteen-year-old boy, related to the Collopys, shot himself in the leg when the firearm he was holding discharged. The teenager claimed to gardaí he was shot in a drive-by shooting, but that scenario was soon refuted.

However, it was an attack on two children that finally caught the attention of the entire nation and brought home to all the serious problems permeating through some of Limerick's estates.

The second weekend in September brought carnage and violence to the upper end of Moyross. The estate was a powder-keg waiting to explode and the events on Sunday, September 10, 2006, were the culmination of trouble that had been brewing over the previous forty-eight hours in the area.

Late on the Friday night, the home of Jenny Shapland, a former Sinn Féin candidate who unsuccessfully ran in the Limerick East by-election in 1998, was fire-bombed. The occupant managed to escape unharmed as flames and black smoke spread downstairs. By the time firemen had secured the burning home, an external wall was damaged along with the lower section of the building.

As firemen tended to the burning property, gardaí received another emergency call. Residents reported joyriding and stolen cars being set alight in a nearby street. Officers responded immediately, but violent mobs lay in wait for them. Gangs of youths, some of whom were as young as thirteen, hid behind walls and houses, ready to 'welcome' the Garda officers with lumps of concrete and petrol bombs. Molotov cocktails were lit and flung at the shocked officers. Somehow, responding gardaí managed to escape unharmed from their night's duty as the gangs slunk back into the shadows.

Saturday arrived, and apprehension gripped residents as darkness fell over the suburb. That night, Moyross resembled a scene from a far-fetched Hollywood set, except this was no film production, but a Limerick-city estate, where the unrelenting violence continued to escalate. A man was stabbed and vandals went on a destructive rampage throughout the northern end of Moyross. Petrol bombs were thrown at houses and into front gardens. Each explosion was met with delighted shouts and whoops from delirious vandals, who rampaged from one street to the next. Terrified residents did not dare open their front doors for fear their house would be attacked or that they would suffer a far worse fate. Again the gardaí were called in and again the gangs, fuelled on a cocktail of drink and drugs, gleefully set about ensnaring and attacking the officers.

Neighbours revealed how gangs of youths stored missiles, weapons and petrol bombs to 'welcome' the emergency services.

'They waited for them in ambush. They had bottles and everything hidden behind walls and in gardens just waiting for them to come up. They just wanted to attack them. They were animals. It is the worst I have ever seen. I don't know what's going on here,' said one resident the following day.

Petrol bombs used were not just the regular bottles filled with fuel and plugged with a piece of paper to act as a fuse. Sugar had been added to the mix as it causes the accelerant to stick to whatever it impacts on and this inflicts even greater damage. Two patrol cars and a Garda van were attacked in the middle of Pineview Gardens by a gang of at least thirty youths. Petrol bombs rained down on the gardaí, and two squad cars were damaged from the missiles. Officers, struggling to control the riot, had to arrest seven people before order could be restored. A special court sitting in the local district court was required on the Sunday.

Twenty-year-old Kenneth Sheehan of Pineview Gardens, Moyross, subsequently pleaded guilty to five charges, including assault, and was sentenced to five months' imprisonment. Sheehan had assaulted Sergeant Eoin Gogarty of Mayorstone Garda station with a brandy bottle as officers attempted to cordon off an area to begin searching for petrol bombs hidden in derelict houses and buildings.

The following morning, the community of Moyross woke up to a bright sunny day, but the scars of the previous two nights' battlegrounds could seen everywhere with the streets and green areas strewn with broken glass and concrete rubble. Charred marks on the ground showed the remnants of the many petrol bombs.

At lunch-time on Sunday, Sheila Murray, a mother-of-eight, left her home with two of her children, six-year-old Philomena, known affectionately as 'Millie', and her four-year-old brother, Gavin. The little boy had just started primary school the week beforehand and was nick-named 'Gummy' by his neighbours as his upper set of teeth had just fallen out.

Sheila drove the short distance from her own end-of-terrace family home to a friend's house in Pineview Gardens. She pulled up and parked her green Toyota Corolla outside the house at 1.40pm and brought the children inside the home with her to visit their neighbours. Sheila and her friend were due to travel across the city to Garryowen, where the father of Millie and Gavin, Niall McNamara, lived with his mother. Inside the house, Sheila accepted the offer of a cup of tea, and Gavin and Millie played patiently, waiting for their mother to bring them to see their dad. As the friends chatted in the kitchen, across the small estate three youths found themselves looking for a lift to the special-court sitting that was taking place in the district courthouse.

Sixteen-year-old Robert Sheehan, seventeen-year-old Jonathan O'Donoghue and a third youth, Mr X, had decided to ask neighbours for a lift to the court. Kenneth Sheehan (older brother of Robert), who had been arrested the night previously, was appearing at the court sitting and Robert wanted to be there for it. All three youths were from Moyross and knew their neighbours and the locality well.

Robert Sheehan had just begun his Junior Certificate year

in the nearby secondary school, St Nessan's Community College, and had just celebrated his sixteenth birthday on the Thursday beforehand. He lived with his mother and three older brothers and one sister in Pineview Gardens. A keen Arsenal fan, he played for Moyross U17 soccer team, and, like a lot of youths in Limerick City, had a great love and interest in horses.

Jonathan O'Donoghue had attended the same secondary school as Sheehan. His parents separated when he was six years old and he lived with his mother, also in Pineview Gardens. His father had moved to England. He was the second eldest of three brothers and three sisters. O'Donoghue was an apprentice carpenter who was described as having a good pair of hands and was on block release from FÁS at the time. The trio spotted Sheila's Toyota Corolla parked outside the her friend's home and decided to ask her for a lift into town.

At 1.45pm, they walked up to the front door, knocked and were met by Sheila's friend. Jonathan O'Donoghue quickly took the initiative and asked for a lift into Limerick courthouse in Sheila's car. Sheila came to the door and immediately noticed that O'Donoghue was 'messing' with her car and that the windows had been rolled down. She said that she could not help the teenagers as she had prior engagements and had to go to Garryowen. The three youths repeated their request and, again, Sheila turned them down.

At this stage, with an empty car at the front entrance to the house, the three youths became aggressive and began shouting abuse at Sheila and threatened to burn out her car. The mother went back inside the house and closed the door on them. O'Donoghue, who did most of the talking at the doorway, was in particularly foul form as the youths walked down to Casey's shop less than a hundred yards in Delmege Park. On the short walk, O'Donoghue informed his companions that he was going to carry out the threat and burn out Sheila Murray's car.

Outside Casey's shop, seventeen-year-old John Mitchell was hanging about and waiting for a game of soccer with local teenagers. Mitchell was later described as an 'exceptionally gifted soccer player', who seemed destined to earn a successful career as a professional soccer player in England. His father worked as a butcher and his mother was also in full-time employment. He was the eldest child in the family and was in his last year in school. John Mitchell had two younger brothers and a sister and lived in Delmege Park. The talented, young athlete was about to embark on a series of trials that September and Mitchell, who had never come to the attention of gardaí or the authorities before, seemed certain to live out a life that most teenage boys could only dream about. Within twenty minutes, John Mitchell's hopes of one day playing at Old Trafford or Anfield were gone forever.

He met the three youths, who relayed their unsuccessful quest to secure a lift to the courthouse. The group then entered Casey's shop and asked for a lift to the court, but again had no success. They began walking back up to Sheila's car. O'Donoghue had now assumed the role as leader of the small group and was intent on swift retribution for Sheila's refusal to oblige the youths. Walking into Pineview Gardens, Mr X left Robert Sheehan while Jonathan O'Donoghue and John Mitchell went into one of the back gardens. They set about preparing a petrol bomb with a plastic Lucozade bottle and magazine paper. Robert Sheehan was standing nearby and acting as lookout. Sheila emerged from the home and placed her two children, Gavin and Millie, into her car. Ironically, despite the events over the previous thirty-six hours, it was a bright afternoon in Moyross and there was no sign of the horror that was about to envelope Pineview Gardens and cast a dark shadow over the lives of two children forever.

Sheila sat into the car with her children behind her and waited for her friend to join them. It was then that Jonathan O'Donoghue threw the lit petrol bomb at the car. It crashed straight in the open back passenger window and exploded. Petrol and flames engulfed the two children as their clothes burned and their skin began to melt. The car burst into flames and the children screamed out in excruciating pain.

Hearing the consternation and the impact from the petrol bomb, residents rushed to the scene. Sheila grabbed her burning daughter and raced into a house screaming for help. Robert Sheehan, who was standing in the vicinity of his own home along with teenagers, Noel Stanners and Ross Kelly, pulled Gavin from the car as his cries pierced the air. Stanners took off his Nike jumper and quenched the flames on Gavin.

Speaking at his home in Delmege Park, Noel Stanners

recalled the incident days later, 'I was just sitting in the garden when it all happened. We just saw a fire and ran over. There was another fella there too, Ross Kelly, he helped us. All we were trying to do was put out the flames on him [Gavin]. Then Rob [Robert Sheehan] picked him up and ran into the neighbour's house with him. He was really screaming.'

Robert Sheehan carried the injured boy into the bathroom and placed him in the sink while Sheila's friend turned on the taps and began to douse the boy in water. Speaking after the incident, Robert Sheehan said: 'His skin was all burnt and marked. There was a smell of burning off him. All his hair was singed and burnt off. His ear was in bits.'

Millie was also treated in the house as they waited for an ambulance before they were rushed to the Mid-Western Regional Hospital in Dooradoyle. The two arsonists fled from the back of the house. Jonathan O'Donoghue raced to the back of Pineview Gardens. A short time later he spoke to residents who informed him two children had been burnt. John Mitchell ran and hid in a shed at a nearby house. After waiting for the commotion to die down, he calmly went home and changed his jumper. Jonathan O'Donoghue collected his pony, met John Mitchell and gave the animal a bucket of water before the pair then decided to go to Barretts' shop on the old Cratloe Road.

Experienced paramedics tending to the children said they never saw anyone in such unbearable pain in the ambulance on the way across the city to the hospital. One medical worker described the incident as 'the most horrible thing I have come across' during thirty years of service.

The following day on *The Gerry Ryan Show* on 2FM, a woman who was visiting a relative in the Limerick hospital, said she never heard such screams of pain in her life when the children were rushed through the Accident and Emergency department. At that stage both were in a critical condition and fighting for their lives.

Staff at the hospital immediately realised the children's lives were in danger and they knew they had to react quickly. Millie had suffered extreme burning to her face, right arm, right thigh and lower back. She had to be resuscitated and incubated. It was later diagnosed that she suffered burns to thirty per cent of her body. She was given pain relief, and a decision was made to transfer her immediately to Our Lady's Hospital for Sick Children in Crumlin. Sheila Murray travelled to Dublin in the Garda car behind the ambulance. The mother had no option but to leave Gavin behind her in Limerick.

Gavin suffered burning to the side of his head, face, back, both hands, right arm and, his right ear had effectively melted away. The little boy was in excruciating agony and was given pain relief and had to be sedated in Limerick. His face was swelling badly and medical staff feared for his life. The burning threatened his airways and his breathing had to be assisted. Twenty-five per cent of the four-year-old's body had been badly burned in the fire. He was rushed to Dublin hours after Millie when it was deemed safe enough for him to make the journey. In Crumlin, the children were both

ventilated. Consultant Plastic Surgeon at the Crumlin hospital Dr David Orr realised that the children had sustained
life-threatening burns and would suffer severe permanent
disfigurement.

In the meantime, a Garda investigation began back in
Limerick. The country was left horrified as details of the
incident emerged and there was intense media focus on
what happened and who was culpable. Investigating gardaí
questioned residents and spoke to John Mitchell and Jonathan O'Donoghue. Two days after the attack, accompanied
with their parents, the pair came to Mayorstone Garda station by appointment and were immediately arrested under
Section 30 of the Offences Against the State Act. They were
questioned on numerous separate occasions and the case
against them arose from the submissions they made.

Jonathan O'Donoghue admitted to being the ringleader
of the group during the course of his seven interviews. After
initially denying his responsibility for the attack and pointing the finger of blame at John Mitchell, O'Donoghue
admitted to throwing the petrol bomb. 'I threw the petrol
bomb, but did not know the kids were in the car,' he said to
officers.

Mitchell was interviewed on ten occasions and a concrete case against the pair was established. Under heavy
media scrutiny, the two were charged before a special sitting of Limerick district court four days after the incident.
They shielded their faces with blankets when being
escorted to and from the courthouse. Jonathan
O'Donoghue had to leave Limerick shortly after the attack

as his life was threatened a number of times. When he achieved bail and awaited trial, he moved to Tipperary for his own safety. He began studying for his Leaving Certificate while in St Patrick's Institution. Robert Sheehan was arrested when he presented himself to gardaí, by appointment, on the same day that Mitchell and O'Donoghue were charged. He was later released, but during the Christmas holidays, he appeared in court in connection with the attack.

Over time, Millie's wounds were reconstructed with skin grafts taken from her back and legs. She was placed in the burns ward in Crumlin after initial treatment and remained there for months, but recovered enough to make a guest appearance on the *Late Late Show*. During the following year, she made an excellent recovery, but the young girl will require further surgery as she grows older.

Her brother could only have burns cleaned under general anaesthetic as his pain was too much. Gavin has been left with permanent facial disfigurement and loss of hair on his scalp. A year after the petrol bombing, a small withered scar remained where his left ear was, and a nurse still had to call to the children's primary school to apply cream to their wounds. The children had to wear protective clothing for their injuries while Gavin had to use an uncomfortable facial shield at night. They are both extremely lucky to be alive.

On February 13, 2007, in Ennis District Court, both John Mitchell and Jonathan O'Donoghue pleaded guilty to their roles in the arson attack. They had been charged with intentionally or recklessly causing serious harm to Gavin and Millie (Philomena) Murray. Robert Sheehan initially pleaded not guilty to the same charge on June 13, and a jury was sworn in to hear his trial. The court heard that his trial could take up to three weeks and more than fifty witnesses, including neighbours, friends, gardaí and journalists who interviewed the teenager after the attack, would be called. Sheehan's legal team went into consultations with the prosecution and, on the second day of the trial, Sheehan agreed to plead guilty to a lesser charge of endangerment.

The subsequent sentencing of the three arsonists was one of the most emotive cases ever heard in Limerick Circuit Criminal Court. It required two sittings, a year after the incident, on September 24 and October 12, 2007. On the morning of September 24, Sheila Murray attended the courthouse with her two children in tow. Both were wearing their Ballynanty primary-school uniforms and bearing the obvious scars from the event which had taken place a year previously.

Prosecuting on behalf of the Director of Public Prosecutions, experienced barrister John O'Sullivan opened the proceedings. Recalling the harrowing incident, the packed courtroom was reduced to silence and tears as evidence was given of the horrific injuries suffered by the children and the unbearable pain cast upon them following the attack. Inspector Seamus Nolan said the children would suffer extensive psychological trauma in future years. Solicitors, barristers and members of the public hid their tears as Sheila Murray told Judge Carroll Moran of the impact the

arson attack had on her children and her family in the subsequent twelve months. Sitting just yards from Sheila, the
three defendants bowed their head and wept into their
hands as Gavin and Millie's mother attempted to fight back
the tears while reading her victim impact statement in the
witness box.

* * *

Sheila Murray read:

On the 10th of September 2006, my life completely
changed, because on this date two of my eight children
were badly burnt by a petrol bomb that was thrown into
my car.

Myself and my children did nothing wrong for this to
happen, only I refused someone a lift to the courthouse.

I left my friend's house with my children and next thing
my car was in flames. I got out and pulled my daughter,
Millie, out of the car and was shouting for help for Gavin.

I couldn't even see Gavin in the car when I got Millie
out because of thick black smoke. I could only see smoke
and flames.

I don't think I will ever get rid of the guilt that I couldn't
get Gavin out with Millie and he might not have been
burnt so bad if I was able to get him.

Doing this victim impact report and coming to the

court lately means I have to start talking about what happened that day and it always makes me feel sick to talk about it, but I have been advised by my psychologist and social worker that it would be better for myself and my children to deal with it.

On that day everything was a daze, but I just kept going and I didn't even know how I did. I had to sit in the back of a guard's car while we followed the ambulance carrying Millie to Dublin and I had to leave Gavin behind in Limerick because he was too bad to travel.

He went straight into intensive care in the regional. Doctors told me the first twenty-four to forty-eight hours were critical for both Millie and Gavin.

But I sat in the intensive care unit with Millie and waited and asked about Gavin.

Nobody was telling me, but I knew Gavin was badly burned because he couldn't be moved. I couldn't be with the two of them and I didn't know if any of them would survive. All I could do was try keep in contact with the Regional in Limerick and try to be there for Millie.

I was so worried I couldn't eat or sleep properly as I didn't know what I would be told next, because I knew both Millie and Gavin were heavily sedated because of the pain and because they needed to breathe.

Life for me for the next few months involved me travelling up and down from Limerick to Dublin, my children being taken care of by myself, friends and family and moving the children from one place to the next. I felt like I was being pulled all over the place between being at the hospital with Millie and Gavin and having to leave them and be there for the rest of my children.

And in the middle of it all, it cost me a fortune coming and going, buying new clothes all the time for Millie and Gavin as most of their clothes and pyjamas had to be cut to get them on and off because of their bandages and then I had to get accommodation, travel and food to pay for.

I felt like my life and my children's lives were all over the place. I just about owned my house in Pineview Gardens as I was buying it from the corporation, but now we no longer live there.

I used to get on with my neighbours and my children had friends there. We had to move and are trying to make a new life in another area.

While I was in Crumlin hospital, I watched Millie and Gavin going through intensive burns treatment every day.

When they were coming off the sedation, they were in terrible pain, but I had to be there to support them along with the medical staff. Most of the time I had to leave the room, because I couldn't stand to watch them any more. I could never go far, though, as I had to be there constantly. Millie and Gavin have had operations, but I have been told they will need a lot more treatment, more skin grafts, and Gavin will need to have his ear fixed.

They will be scarred physically for the rest of their lives and apart from the psychological effects it has had and will have on them.

Myself and all my children are having counselling because of all this. Since Millie and Gavin came out of hospital in January they have their dressings/creams done by nurses every second day and physio three times a week.

They have to wear special 'jobst garments' all over their burns. Gavin has one for his back, neck and his head as most of his burns are on his head. The children complain about wearing them as they are very uncomfortable, especially in the warm weather, and I have a constant fight to get them to wear them.

Our whole lives now revolve around Millie and Gavin's treatment. We can't go anywhere or arrange anything like a break away for them or the rest of the children because of their treatment.

I have to sit up most nights with Gavin as he gets bad nightmares. They are both frightened to sleep on their own so they sleep with me.

The rest of my children have all been affected too. They missed a lot of school, being upset, had to move house and seen and heard what was going on.

They visited their brother and sister in hospital and know what they have gone through. They have also missed out as most of the time I couldn't be with them because of having to travel up and down to Dublin. Our lives will never be the same again and Millie and Gavin will never get their full health back. They are scarred for the rest of their lives.

I will think of that day every time I look at my children. I try to go around as normal, but every day it just gets harder. We lost our home and our lives have been turned upside down.

* * *

Family members of the three defendants were also visibly upset when Ms Murray finished reading, and a deafening silence filled the visibly-shaken court room.

From the publicity the incident received, and following Millie's TV appearance on the *Late Late Toy Show* nine months beforehand, Judge Carroll Moran said it was completely unrealistic to impose reporting restrictions on the case regarding the children. He also deemed it in the public's best interest that Robert Sheehan's name could be published, despite the fact that he was seventeen years old and legally underage at the time of sentencing. The decision to adjourn sentencing until October 12 was met with sighs of disapproval from the families and friends of all, but Judge

Moran insisted he needed time to consider such a serious matter.

The fate of the three accused teenagers was made known on a grey Friday morning with the nation's media looking on. Again, there was further drama in the court case. Judge Moran said he must consider mitigating factors before deciding what sentence was appropriate to each person. He noted that the arson attack happened against a backdrop of petrol bombs being thrown in the area throughout the weekend and said the arson attack was 'not feud-related'. The judge said the three accused pleaded guilty at early points and that the prosecution case was based entirely on their admissions. The judge said the guilty pleas were an acknowledgement to the Murray/McNamara family and society at large that the three have done wrong. The court heard that gardaí accepted the three teenagers did not know the two children were in the car.

Judge Moran said the gratuitous nature of the offence was appalling, 'Throwing petrol bombs around is bad enough, but to do so for such a trifling reason for not getting a lift into town elevates this offence into anarchic nihilism. The casualness of this offence strikes all of us.'

Jonathan O'Donoghue, who Judge Moran regarded as the 'main mover' in the affair, was sentenced to eight years' imprisonment with two years suspended and backdated to June 30, 2007. He had four previous convictions, including offences for obstructing a member of the gardaí and stealing a car.

Talented soccer player, John Mitchell received seven

years' imprisonment with two years also suspended. The sentence was backdated to September 14, 2007 and he was allowed to complete his Leaving Certificate as requested by probation officers.

Robert Sheehan, whose role was regarded as a 'considerably less' one by the presiding judge, received a two-year sentence and was bound to the peace for four years. In February 2009, the then eighteen-year-old Sheehan was sentenced to fourteen months' imprisonment for a plethora of offences committed over the previous ten months, including possession of a knife and dangerous driving. When he was locked up in 2009, despite his young age, Robert Sheehan had amassed forty-eight previous convictions.

The attack on the two children was not gang- or feud-related, but it was the activities of the gangs and drug dealing which had allowed estates in Moyross to descend into such conflict.

Speaking in her home after the case to *RTÉ News*, Sheila Murray said her children had a long road of recovery ahead: 'People are saying to me all day "it is over with now don't worry, it is over with like", but it's not. It's over in the courts, but it's not over for us, not for a long time, and the kids still have to get treatment for years so how is it over?'

Sitting with her two children beside her, Sheila Murray looked down as her children played for cameramen. 'I can pull a skid on a scooter, look,' Gavin proudly said, before displaying his skills, content in the knowledge he was at home with his older sister. His innocence is a glaring contrast to what was happening in Limerick. What happened was a result of the breakdown in society – beyond the feud, beyond the gangs. Life in parts of Limerick was crumbling at the seams; Judge Carroll Moran described it as 'anarchic nihilism'. Whatever solution might be found for dealing with Limerick's feuding gangs, it will not solve the damage to normal functioning society as easily.

11

Boy Shot & Uncle Murdered

Moyross and Limerick were still reeling at the appalling arson attack on the two children a week after it took place. In the immediate aftermath of the attack, an extra sixteen gardaí were sent to Limerick's troubled estates and the public condemnation of the young culprits continued. However, the presence of the extra officers was not enough to deter further bloodshed in Moyross and, a week later, a young criminal from the suburb was shot dead.

Frank Ryan hailed from Delmege Park and the twenty-one-year-old was better known as 'Fat Frankie', due to his rotund appearance. Fat Frankie openly associated with the McCarthy/Dundon gang and was one of their key men on the northside of the city. He knew Moyross intimately and was well aware that he had made enemies for himself across the city, most notably in his home estate, where a rival gang enviously eyed the control he exercised for the McCarthy/Dundons.

Fat Frankie had amassed eleven previous convictions, including public order, robbery, theft and road-traffic offences. Fat Frankie was never far from trouble and he was understood to have been involved in a number of shooting incidents in the city during the violent summer months of 2006. He was also questioned after the murder of Aidan Kelly in Blackwater, County Clare, as officers attempted to see could the young Limerick man shed any light on how Kelly died. Kelly's assailants also attempted to murder Fat Frankie on the same night in the quiet countryside, but he jumped over a ditch and escaped. Fat Frankie had been scheduled to appear in the local district court on September 18. He had applied to have a car returned to him from the gardaí. Detectives had seized the car, the previous year, during their investigations into the death of David Nunan and suspected that Fat Frankie had been involved in the murder.

Fat Frankie had been hauled in for questioning by gardaí on a number of occasions, in relation to other offences. Despite this, he attempted to intimidate law officers and would follow them home at the end of their shifts, letting them know he knew where they lived.

At 10.45pm, on the night of September 17, and a week after the petrol-bomb attack on Gavin and Millie Murray, Fat Frankie Ryan was driving between Pineview Gardens and Delmege Park and chatting to a seventeen-year-old friend, who he had collected in Delmege Park. They drove around the corner and picked up a well-known Limerick criminal who had just been released from prison less than forty-eight hours earlier. The meeting between Fat Frankie and the Limerick man was meant to be a cordial affair to discuss future ventures, but in true Limerick criminal style, it turned out to be a lethal double-cross. Unknown to Fat Frankie, or his friend, their criminal associate sitting in the back-seat was armed with a handgun. They had only gone a short distance when he put the gun to the back of Fat Frankie's head and shot the driver at point-blank range. The car stopped between Delmege Park and Pineview Gardens as blood poured from the driver's mouth and nose. The gunman got out and fired a second shot into the Moyross criminal's head as he lay motionless. Fat Frankie Ryan died instantly. His executioner ran from the scene shouting that if anyone 'ratted' or talked about what happened, 'they were dead'.

The following morning, Limerick awoke to find its northside suburb of Moyross at the centre of an intense media storm for the second successive Monday. It was clear from years of neglect and deprivation, elements in Moyross had descended into a chasm of violence and carnage and were in danger of dragging an entire neighbourhood with them.

Residents in Pineview Gardens and Delmege Park were reluctant to talk about the latest murder in the area.

'Yeah, it is awful, everybody knows that. But what do you want me to say. I open my mouth and next time they come after me. Yeah, the guards are here now, but there was nobody there last night when "Fat Frankie" got it. They can't watch everything,' said one resident in an interview with this author.

In the meantime, the violence and gun crime continued. Two days after the murder of Fat Frankie Ryan, his gang, the McCarthy/Dundons, was involved in a high-speed shootout in Ballyneety, County Limerick. Apprentice carpenter, twenty-year-old Paul Reddan from Delmege Park, a member of the criminal gang, was driving his Volkswagen Passat to the east Limerick town of Bruff to collect associates who were involved in the city's feud and due to appear before Bruff district court.

On the journey to Bruff, Reddan, now in the company of the two other criminals, came up behind a hiace van which was being driven by Willie Moran from St Mary's Park with Sean Keane – Christy and Kieran Keane's brother – in the passenger seat. In broad daylight, the front-seat passenger in the Passat emerged from his window and opened fire at the van travelling in front of them. Keane jumped into the back of the van to see who was shooting at them, but had to lie on the floor of the vehicle when three shots were fired at the van. One of the gun blasts came through the back window and hit the sun visor in the front of the van. During the chase, Reddan attempted to overtake the van, but Moran quickly swerved across the road to block his path. Willie Moran drove frantically to Ballyneety Garda station, while the Passat continued on in the direction of Bruff, but not before they had passed an alert Detective Sergeant Con McCarthy who noted their registration plate. Reddan was arrested later that day in Ballinacurra Weston.

At his subsequent court case in February 9, 2007, Reddan pleaded guilty to possession of a firearm and control of ammunition with intent to endanger life. The gun used was never recovered and Reddan's two companions were never apprehended.

Detective Dave Bourke said Reddan was not a leading member of the McCarthy/Dundon gang but 'is well involved in the feud especially in transportation'.

Prosecution counsel, John O'Sullivan compared the incident 'to the old style gangster films out of Chicago'.

Judge Carroll Moran said Reddan allowed himself to be used in the incident and it was 'a lucky miracle that Mr Keane was not killed'. The judge maintained the defendant may not be a leading member of the McCarthy/Dundon gang, but pointed out that he was 'not on the periphery either' and sentenced Reddan to five years in prison.

As a result of the shooting, Reddan's parents and his brother had to flee their Moyross home after it was shot at following the high-speed shooting. Reddan's car was also targeted in another gun attack.

Against this backdrop of violence, the funeral of Fat Frankie took place. If the level of intense hatred that the feuding gangs had for each other was still not apparent, it became crystal clear at the funeral service. With the grieving Ryan family and Fat Frankie's neighbours and friends gathered in front of him, Corpus Christi Parish Priest, Fr Frank O'Dea appealed for no retaliation attacks. 'Revenge and retaliation is futile. It is not the way forward. Those who seek revenge take the path of weakness,' Fr O'Dea said.

Armour-plated and bullet-proof BMW, belonging to the Dundons, which was seized by CAB.

Wayne Dundon.

Kenneth Dundon.

John Dundon.

Above: Dessie Dundon.

Right: Brian Fitzgerald.

Left: Anthony 'Noddy' McCarthy.

Bottom left: John Creamer.

Bottom right: James McCarthy.

Above: Shane Geoghegan.

Right: Ger Dundon.

Two rifles (one with a silencer attached), a pump-action shotgun, telescopic sights, 150 rounds of ammunition and cocaine worth €150,000, belonging to one of Limerick's gangs in Roxboro Garda station on November 28, 2008.

Left: Ibrihme Hassan.

Below: Remington bolt-action precision rifle found in the home of Peter O'Brien on September 30, 2006.

The murder scene following shooting of Noel Campion in Thomondgate on April 26, 2007.

Right: Roy Collins.

Below: March of concerned citizens in Limerick, following the death of Roy Collins, May 2009.

Above: Philip Collopy's funeral procession on March 25, 2009.

Right: Philip Collopy.

Below: A Toyota Dyna van leading Philip Collopy's funeral procession on March 25, 2009.

John Fitzgerald.

Michael Murray.

House demolition in Pineview Gardens, Moyross.

Within moments, it became clear that his appeals had fallen on deaf ears as a chilling message was read out at the end of the funeral service which promised further violence and a fight to the end between the city's feuding gangs. A poem entitled, 'In memory of a true friend' was read out by twenty-year-old Peter O'Brien, a neighbour and childhood friend of the dead man:

God above in heaven, why did his life end?
Why did you let them take my friend?
All we know now is a fight to the end.
We have written this letter but have no address.
Frankie, my brother, we are all left in a mess.
We don't know what to say, but we all know what to do.
Everything we do, we will think of you.

The poem was signed from: Noddy, Christopher, Gareth, Wayne, John, Dessie and David. A floral wreath, 'Frankie loves Dundon boys', was paraded at the front of the cortege on its journey across the city. It was quite clear who the dead man's loyalty had been with.

On September 23, a rally against antisocial behaviour in Moyross attracted 150 people to City Hall. Nevertheless, the shootings continued the same weekend with at least five incidents in Moyross and reports of gangs openly shooting at each other in the middle of the road, making it the third weekend of violence in the suburb. The night after the rally, in Delmege Park, forty-two-year-old Jenny Shapland and a fourteen-year-old boy were both shot. Shapland suffered injuries to her back and legs, while the boy received wounds to his legs. The previous July, Shapland's twenty-two-year-old son Shane was jailed for five years for shooting at a Garda patrol car. The patrol car was attending the scene of a crash when three uniformed gardaí came under attack at Ballygrennan Close, Moyross, on May 18, 2004. Shane was armed with a sawn-off shotgun and pleaded guilty at Limerick Circuit Court to possession of a sawn-off shotgun with intent to endanger life. Gardaí, supported by the ERU, recovered thirteen firearms and a substantial quantity of ammunition in Moyross over a three-week period, but the sheer defiance of the gangs continued to account for the ongoing violence and shootings.

After he read out the warning poem at the funeral mass of 'Fat Frankie', Peter O'Brien was forced to leave his home at Delmege Park out of fear for his girlfriend and child. The young man, who had never been in trouble before, was afraid of being targeted by rivals of his dead friend and armed himself with a Remington bolt-action precision rifle. On September 30, Detectives Sean Lynch and Mark Deasy searched O'Brien's home, found the rifle and eleven rounds of ammunition, and he was arrested and charged.

At his trial the following year, the court heard that Peter O'Brien was asked by the Ryan family to read out the poem at the funeral mass. Detective Lynch explained that as a result of the attention he drew to himself by reading out the poem, Peter O'Brien felt under great threat from 'certain individuals' and had the rifle for his own protection. The firearm was worth €10,000 and had a telescopic sight worth €4,000. Detective Lynch told the court that the rifle was capable of inflicting fatal injuries on somebody within a one-mile radius. Peter O'Brien, who came from a good family and held down steady employment, was sentenced to two years' imprisonment in 2007, but this was doubled the following year by the Court of Criminal Appeal who found the imprisonment term unduly lenient.

Less than a month after the petrol bomb scarred her children for life, Sheila Murray fled her home in Pineview Gardens, Moyross when it came under attack from a gang who threw rocks and bricks at her windows in the early hours of October 8. The following night in Delmege Park, a twenty-year-old was shot in the head and suffered pellet-gun wounds to the face from a gunman, who opened fire with a shotgun from a passing car. It was only a matter of time before the escalating violence would result in further loss of life.

Gardaí reacted swiftly and, on October 10, officers armed with a search warrant entered a house in Delmege Park, where they found an assortment of weapons and ammunition, including an Israeli-manufactured Desert Eagle handgun, an American-manufactured Ruger SP101.357 Magnum and various rounds of ammunition. Inside the house was the seventeen-year-old brother of Fat Frankie, Gerard Ryan, who was holding the Desert Eagle gun in his right hand and a magazine clip in his left hand. He threw both items on the couch and tried to sit on top of them, hiding them when gardaí entered the house. Ryan told officers he bought the handgun complete with ammunition for €3,000 for his own protection after his older brother was assassinated. He said he purchased the gun from a man in town after he was given his phone number.

In the Circuit Criminal Court, Gerard Ryan pleaded guilty to having the handgun and ten rounds of .9mm ammunition and was sentenced to five years' imprisonment backdated to the time of the offence in 2007.

Gardaí found the silver Ruger handgun in a coal bag behind the front door of the house, and a sixteen-year-old boy who was in the house said he bought the Ruger gun the morning of the raid at Moyross soccer pitch and had it for his protection as people in the suburb wanted to kill him. He spent more than a year in custody before he was freed and ordered to obey all directions of the probation service.

Two other brothers were also found at the house. Alan Kelly, aged nineteen, of Delmege Park, pleaded guilty to possession of thirty-two bullets. The later court sitting heard that Alan Kelly signed a statement 'AK-47'. During interviews with Sergeant Paul Ryan of Mayorstone Garda station, Alan Kelly said he was not worried about the house at Delmege Park being left open during the day as it was only at night 'they shoot you'. Sergeant Ryan said Alan Kelly was very good friends with Fat Frankie Ryan and had become involved in the feuding since his murder. When asked was he concerned about the children's safety in Moyross, if they were to get caught in the crossfire, Alan Kelly replied: 'I wouldn't give a fuck if a child was shot in the middle of the road ... I've nothing to lose, I don't give a fuck about anyone. I'd love a shoot-out with Mr X; a couple of hours before he shot Frankie, he said he'd shoot me.'

Alan Kelly was subsequently sentenced to four years' imprisonment a year later.

Alan's older brother, twenty-one-year-old Gary Kelly, also from Delmege Park, pleaded guilty to possession of forty-five rounds of ammunition. He was sentenced to two years' imprisonment. Passing sentence, Judge Carroll Moran said Gary Kelly was dragged into the matter and allowed his house to be used.

The day after the raid, the Defence Force's bomb-disposal team carried out a controlled explosion on a grenade which was discovered nearby. A week later, on the evening of October 16, before he presented his morning radio show from Moyross Community Centre, RTÉ broadcaster Pat Kenny came to Limerick and went on a stroll of Pineview Gardens. He was approached by a teenager who showed Kenny that he was armed with a semi-automatic Mauser pistol while other teenagers nearby were wearing bullet-proof vests.

The situation in Limerick had become too much and the government had to react. On a tour of Moyross in October, Justice Minister Michael McDowell revealed that the government would appoint a 'national-standing figure' to tackle social disorder in the city's estates.

Over the bank holiday weekend of October 2006, it was announced that former Dublin City Manager, John Fitzgerald was to address crime and social problems in Moyross. Appointed Dublin City manager in 1996, Fitzgerald had overseen radical changes in Dublin. The capital's city centre had been falling into decline as residents deserted the city for the suburbs. Fitzgerald is widely credited for transforming and revitalising Dublin City centre and some of its slums and derelict areas.

Tackling Moyross, Fitzgerald was initially set to report to the Cabinet Committee on Social Exclusion, but his remit would soon expand. He set about a speedy investigation of the issues affecting the northside suburb and other parts of Limerick City and was due to report back to the government in early 2007. It only became clear as time progressed that this was not another false dawn and Fitzgerald represented the first real hope for Limerick's beleaguered estates.

If Fitzgerald was in any doubt of the task that awaited him, he got a swift reminder just twenty-four hours after his appointment was made public. Four successive nights of violence across Limerick began on Hallowe'en night when arsonists attacked the Delmege Park family home of Fat Frankie and a nearby house. Nobody was harmed. The following night, gardaí had to preserve two scenes in Southill after separate gun and arson attacks. On the third night, two drive-by shootings took place in O'Malley Park, Southill. One of the homes targeted was where thirty-two-year-old Paul Crawford, an associate of the McCarthy/Dundon gang, lived with his family.

Crawford, a well-built man, had become an open target in the gangland feud. He had over twenty convictions, dating back to 1986 and included public-order and motoring offences. Crawford was regarded by gang figures from the Island Field (St Mary's Park) as a 'legitimate target' in the feud. Seventeen bullets were sprayed into the family home on November 2, and children in the room narrowly avoided death. Windows, photo frames and the inside walls bore testimony to the attack on the terraced house. The same evening another house was also fire-bombed in the southside estate.

On November 3, Paul Crawford was walking through John Carew Park, Southill, when a stolen Hyundai Sports Coupe with four occupants pulled up alongside him and a shotgun emerged from the car and was pointed at him. The gun jammed and Crawford escaped.

The car took off in the direction of Childers' Road and fired a single shot at a man near Our Lady of Lourdes' Church in Ballinacurra Weston. The passengers then proceeded to dump the weapon at the Crescent Shopping Centre, while members of the Emergency Response Unit gave chase in a four-by-four jeep. The pursuit continued out onto the main Cork-Limerick Road, reaching speeds of 150mph, before the Hyundai was forced off the road at Banogue, County Limerick. One of the four arrested at the scene was a fifteen-year-old youth.

On the evening of November 5, a sixteen-year-old was arrested on board a city-bound Bus Éireann bus from Moyross. When arrested the youth was found in possession of a Beretta double-barrel, sawn-off shotgun and five shotgun cartridges.

The same day, the feud in Limerick reached a new low when a five-year-old boy was shot outside his home. Jordan Crawford, the nephew of Paul Crawford, was standing near his uncle when a gunman opened fire on the home with a hand-held machine gun. The little boy was shot in the right leg. The bullet from the machine gun went clean through his thigh, leaving an entry and exit wound. Not realising he had been shot, the child raced back into his home before he started screaming in pain.

His mother, Olivia Crawford, recalled to this author: 'After the shooting I didn't realise he had been shot. He was crying, but I thought it was from the shock of the bang from the gun. I thought he was frightened. It was a minute or two before we realised what had happened. It was terrible seeing him lying on the floor with the blood coming from his leg. He was wearing his pyjamas and was just about to go to bed.'

Jordan was operated on and recovered from the shooting in the Sunshine Ward of the Mid-Western Regional Hospital.

After the incident, Paul Crawford admitted to this author that he was the gunman's intended target as he was friends with members of the McCarthy/Dundon gang.

'They came in here to get me, to finish me off. They wanted me dead and shot my nephew. There is a hit out on me. They want me dead,' he explained to reporters after the attack. He could offer no explanation as to why the gunman attempted to murder him.

However, further horror was to visit the Crawford family the week before Christmas 2006.

At 2.50am, on the night of December 17/18, Noel Crawford, a father-of-six, called to his family home to celebrate his fortieth birthday. While at the house Noel Crawford was standing near the entrance when he was shot in the stomach by a suspected assailant in the street. He died in Paul's arms.

Paul Crawford had avoided another attempt on his life, but his brother Noel paid the ultimate price. In June, 2009, a seventeen-year-old was charged with the murder of Crawford. Investigating officers are also understood to be looking for another young Limerick man for the murder.

Hours after his brother was murdered, Paul Crawford threatened to kill a neighbour outside her home. Gardaí were searching a house at O'Malley Park when Crawford walked past and started to threaten the woman. Crawford pointed at her house and homes on either side of it and said: 'That will be done tonight, children and all, that one as well and that one too. My brother Noel is dead, ye are all dead too.'

He was arrested, brought before court, charged and held in custody. The neighbour later said she wanted to withdraw her statement, which she claimed she made to gardaí while 'totally stressed out'. In response, Detective David Bourke told the judge that the woman had been bullied into withdrawing her statement by the McCarthy/Dundons.

Paul Crawford was sentenced for the threat to kill the following February in Limerick District Court. Defence solicitor, Ted McCarthy said his client was in a state of shock after his brother was shot dead. Judge O'Donnell said the circumstances of which the threats were made were very serious, but gave Crawford credit for pleading guilty and sentenced him to eight months' imprisonment.

Shortly after the attack on Jordan Crawford, twenty-two-year-old Liam Keane was sentenced to three months' imprisonment after he threatened to 'kick the shit' out of a detective garda on January 19, 2006. Keane had just been released from custody at Henry Street Garda station when he proceeded to abuse and make derogatory remarks about members of the gardaí in the station. Detective Pádraig Sutton was standing nearby in plain clothes and had identified himself to Keane before Keane became abusive to the officer. Keane called the officer a bastard, ran into the middle of the street and stopped traffic, before shouting, 'Come and take me on without your uniform and gun, you prick. I'll kick the shit out of you.' He then made off down Henry Street.

On the night of November 12/13, another man was murdered in Southill. Chronic heroin user, twenty-six-year-old Thomas Moran from O'Malley Park was shot dead and his body found in Ashe Avenue, John Carew Park. The murder incident was not connected to the city's feud, but one theory that gardaí investigated is that Moran may have been shot after he attacked the home of a drug dealer who had refused to give him a free fix of heroin. To date, there has been no one charged in connection with Moran's murder.

Less than a year after vile treatment had been meted out to Garda officers responding to a 999 call for an unconscious teenage boy, emergency services were attacked again in O'Malley Park on November 16. A gang of youths armed with a baseball bat set upon two paramedics responding to a call about a fourteen-year-old girl, who was wandering the estate in a drunken state. When they reached the scene, the ambulance was surrounded by the gang and three teenagers attacked the crew. They kicked, punched, spat and threw rocks at the EMT workers and attempted to drag one of them over a nearby wall. The HSE workers managed to retreat to their vehicle where they radioed gardaí for assistance and left the estate.

Despite the focus on the area and the constant presence of armed gardaí, the shootings continued in O'Malley Park and another spate of violence occurred on the night of November 19.

The ghastly night began, at 1am, when a twenty-four-year-old returning from a christening was shot in the neck and leg. The victim had been shot at ten times and was lucky to escape more serious injury. Despite the presence of armed patrols and the Emergency Response Unit, the violence continued. At 3.24am, a house was petrol-bombed with a nearby home shot at minutes later. Perched on the upstairs window of his home, a gunman from a major gang opened fire at his neighbour. At least six shots were fired with gardaí forced to take cover behind walls. When officers went to arrest the suspected gunman, they were challenged by a gang of twenty youths who flung bottles and stones at them.

Throughout November 2006, gun crime continued to rage on the other side of the city in Moyross. Some of the incidents were not officially reported to gardaí, but residents told of nights when homes and cars were targeted by automatic gunfire. For the most part, Delmege Park, where

160 properties were situated, suffered the most serious incidents of gun crime. Over forty of the houses were, by now, vacant, burnt-out or boarded-up. Since September of that year when the arson attack on the Murray children took place, over twenty-five shooting incidents occurred in Moyross. Most Irish towns with a similar population would not have that many incidents of gun crime in 100 years, let alone two months.

At 2.20am, on November 23, Fat Frankie's brother, John Ryan escaped without injury when a single shot from a handgun was fired into his home. The following day, a bomb disposal team travelled to O'Malley Park to deal with a live grenade found in a house there.

At this stage, it was clear that a new scourge had hit Limerick's streets. Before the end of November 2006, gardaí had seized over €1m worth of heroin in the city. Previously, heroin had not been regarded as a popular drug amongst the city's users, but Limerick now had hundreds of heroin addicts. The McCarthy/Dundons and the Keanes were dealing in the dangerous narcotic, and the situation was fuelling the ongoing warfare between the city's gangs.

Twenty-year-old Denis Kelly, who was living in St Munchin's Street, St Mary's Park, was sentenced to six years' imprisonment for transporting heroin worth €400,000 from Dublin to Limerick in 2006. The drugs were found wrapped in three packages underneath the floor of the Toyota Corolla van he was driving. Before he sentenced Denis Kelly, Judge Carroll Moran heard the young man was in fear of his life.

Gardaí and the Health Service Executive also encountered many cases where heroin users from the surrounding counties of Clare, Tipperary and Kerry travelled to Limerick to buy the lethal drug. The city was effectively a centralised distribution point for anyone wishing to buy heroin.

It was against this background in late 2006 that monks from the Franciscan Friars of the Renewal visited Moyross and, undeterred from what they encountered in the area, decided to open their first Irish friary in the heart of the troubled suburb. The order already had set up friaries in some of the toughest neighbourhoods in the world with bases in the Bronx and Harlem boroughs of New York and also in London, Honduras and Albuquerque. The monks residing in Delmege Park were actively engaged in organising community events.

After the murder of Noel Crawford, Defence Minister Willie O'Dea went on local radio station, Limerick's Live 95FM, where he was inundated with calls from irate Moyross and Southill residents, following successive months of violence in their communities. The Limerick politician rejected demands to deploy the army in the estates and urged residents not to resort to drastic measures, such as asking vigilantes, or the IRA, to patrol the estates. According to O'Dea, the problems in Moyross and Southill were complex and authorities needed time to formulate a plan. He also announced that John Fitzgerald's authority was extended from Moyross to include Southill. O'Dea said the government would not be forced to make any decisions by the city's gangs. He maintained: 'Bringing in the army is virtually the last resort. They are there to back up the gardaí. Bringing them in is an admission of a breakdown of law and order, that the gardaí couldn't control the situation. I am not going to let these thugs make me bring in the army and enforce marshal law.'

The year ended on a familiar note with another attempt on a man's life. On December 20, Brian Collopy, whose home in Fedamore had been seized and sold by the Criminal Assets Bureau, was shot twice in Old Francis Street near the city centre, while visiting an associate. The gunman's bullets struck the thirty-four-year-old in the ankle and the thigh and he was rushed to St John's Hospital, but the wounds were not life-threatening.

12

High Street Ambush

It was widely hoped that 2007 would herald the first signs of change in Limerick as authorities and leaders attempted to free communities from the intense hatred of rival gangs and the effects their activities were having on thousands of honest, hard-working people. John Fitzgerald was busy visiting all areas of the city in the first three months, to compile his extensive report and recommendations for the government.

However, the year began in the same fashion as the last one ended with gun attacks in St Brendan Street, St Mary's Park and Cliona Park, Moyross. Lunchtime motorists approaching the city on a busy Friday afternoon had to swerve for cover as a high speed shoot-out took place on the Ennis to Limerick dual carriageway. The drama unfolded, at 1.30pm on January 12, when a gunman emerged from a Volkswagen Passat near Setright's Cross and opened fire on a car ahead. The occupant of the targeted car was a member of the McCarthy/Dundon gang and was returning from a court sitting in Ennis when he was ambushed by the waiting Passat. The shoot-out continued for two-and-a-half miles on the N18 with at least ten shots fired. Frightened motorists narrowly missed being struck or involved in a serious accident. It ended when the gunman's car crashed into perimeter railings near the Radisson Hotel and the occupants fled on foot.

Tensions in Moyross remained high and, on January 18, Karl Shapland – the son of Jenny who was targeted months earlier – was shot twice by a gunman as he stood in his kitchen in Pineview Gardens, Moyross. His injuries were not life-threatening.

The violence continued across the same suburbs and, on February 24, a grenade exploded outside a home in O'Malley Park, leaving a crater in the ground. The house had also been shot at and had a petrol bomb thrown into it hours beforehand but no one was injured. Seven years since the feud first erupted in a bloody death, it showed no signs of ending.

By this point in 2007, the McCarthy/Dundon gang had their sights firmly set on one particular target – Noel Campion. The thirty-five-year-old came from a ruthless and violent family.

His brother, Willie Campion, was convicted of the 1998 murder of sixty-eight-year-old farmer, Patrick (Paud) Skehan at Ard na Taggle, Bridgetown, O'Brien's Bridge,

County Clare. The elderly farmer was beaten by his assailants, before they blindfolded him, tied his limbs together and hung him upside down from the banisters of the stairs with a television cable and doused him in petrol. They left the pensioner for dead. He was found by a neighbour but later died from his injuries. Shoe-prints found in the victim's blood on the floor boards matched those of Willie Campion's shoes and he was sentenced to life imprisonment. The Court of Criminal Appeal later upheld the conviction.

Noel was married with two children. In a long criminal career, he set out as a young man, robbing cars and driving into the countryside, to attack vulnerable elderly people and farmers. In 1999, he received a fourteen-year sentence with six years suspended for the armed robbery of an Emo Oil depot in the city. After release, he was jailed again for six months for a public-order offence and was also connected to dissident republicans. Noel wanted to set up his own criminal enterprise in Moyross and paid no heed to the McCarthy/Dundons or Keanes – opposing gangs with whom he had dealings in the past.

The McCarthy/Dundons held a close associate of Noel Campion's responsible for the murder of Fat Frankie Ryan in September 2006 and wanted bloody revenge. Aware that their every move was being monitored, the gang attempted to force twenty-four-year-old Andrew Ryan, from Pineview Gardens, to carry out the hit on Noel Campion. Ryan, a father-of-two, was spotted by gardaí outside Campion's home in Moyross on March 11, 2007. He attempted to run from the area, but was pursued by officers and arrested. A

Walther PKK semi-automatic pistol was found in his track-suit pocket with six bullets in the magazine. When questioned by gardaí about who supplied him with the weapon, Ryan replied, 'I might as well kill myself if I tell you.' He told officers that the gun was to be used to shoot Noel Campion the next time he saw him. Ryan himself had been in a dispute with Campion and shots had been fired at his Pineview Gardens home shortly before his arrest. Ryan appeared before Judge Carroll Moran in court in December and pleaded guilty to the firearm and ammunition charges.

The judge said he accepted that Ryan had himself been the target of a feared gang and gave him credit for co-operating with gardaí and the guilty plea. 'Even while the accused said to gardaí that he did not intend to kill the person [Noel Campion], he was given it for that instruction,' Judge Moran noted, before sentencing Ryan to six years' imprisonment.

On March 22, 2007, an attempt was made on Noel Campion's life when he was targeted by a lone gunman as he walked near his home in Moyross. Two shots were fired at the thirty-five-year-old, but he escaped. Before the end of the month, Campion had to fork out over €6,000 for the return of six horses, which had been seized by Limerick City Council contractors when it was learned that the animals were being kept illegally in stables at the back of a house in Pineview Gardens, Moyross. Campion had survived a number of attacks at this stage, but his luck was about to run out.

On the morning of April 26, a bright sun beamed down

over Limerick City. It was a clear day. At 10.40am, in Thomondgate, elderly men and women were making their way down High Street and New Road to the local post-office to collect their pensions. Pedestrians were strolling along the river front and taking in the views of the Treaty Stone and King John's Castle, while traffic slowly ambled towards the city.

Noel Campion was on his way to the district court, where he was due to appear for traffic offences and was riding pillion passenger on a motorcycle. After the recent attacks on his life, he had taken to wearing a bulletproof jacket, but had deemed it not necessary to do so this morning. Unknown to Campion, and those in Thomondgate that morning, two men were loitering near two Eircom phone boxes at the junction of Inglewood Terrace, Treaty Terrace and High Road. The motorbike approached High Road to drive towards the city courthouse but, within seconds, all hell erupted as Campion was targeted by a gunman, wearing a red hoodie, who emerged from one of the phone boxes. The assassin opened fire and the high-powered, blue-and-white Suzuki motorcycle crashed into a parked Nissan Primera car in front of it. The motorbike driver went flying into the windscreen. Showing no sympathy, the gunman continued firing at close range as Campion desperately attempted to run away, while petrified motorists looked on. Severely wounded, he fell to the ground opposite an off-licence, less than fifteen yards from where the bike had crashed. Terrified residents peered through their windows and front doors. Emergency services rushed across the Shannon river and brought the married father-of-two to St John's Hospital, but he died shortly after the shooting. He was hit three times, once in the back and on either side.

After the shooting, the culprit ran to Canon Breen Park to a waiting Volkswagen Passat and escaped via New Road, Quarry Road, Ballynanty Road and Moylish Avenue, before ending up in Dalgish Park in the Moyross area, where an attempt was made to burn out the stolen 1998 Galway-registered vehicle. Superintendent John Kerin appealed for anyone who saw the culprits make their getaway in the stolen car to contact gardaí immediately.

While officers cordoned off the murder scene, one resident said he was in bed when he heard the gunfire. 'I heard the six shots: bang, bang, bang, bang, bang, bang. They were like mad wallops. I ran upstairs, I knew they were gunshots and there was a girl standing over the man screaming. He was just lying there on the ground still wearing the motorcycle helmet. This is all feud-related. Please don't use my name.'

One of the dead man's sisters, twenty-three-year-old Mary Campion, having spent the morning shopping in the city centre, happened upon the scene in a taxi accompanied by her thirty-three-year-old friend Shirley Bourke. Both women claimed to gardaí they saw Kieran 'Rashers' Ryan, the son of murdered Eddie Ryan, armed with a handgun running away from the scene. They later admitted to making a false statement to gardaí concerning the alleged identity of the gunman. When their case came before the courts, Detective Thelma Watters acknowledged that both women had come under pressure from a third party and later admitted they had lied. The court outcome showed that Kieran 'Rashers' Ryan was not connected in any way to Campion's murder.

If the scenes in Thomondgate on the morning of Noel Campion's murder were not bad enough, they got uglier across Limerick as darkness descended. The McCarthy/Dundon gang and their associates openly celebrated the murder with late-night parties. Young children wore T-shirts with mottos commemorating the atrocity in both Southill and Weston.

'Whack, whack, Noely got it in the back' and 'Noely pissed himself when he was shot in the back' were some of the slogans. In O'Malley Park, Southill, celebrators gathered around a bonfire on a green area and passed the night away in a drunken and drugged haze. Shouts of 'Holy Noely' could be heard from passing vehicles in Hyde Road. Later that night, a sixteen-year-old youth was shot by a man armed with a shotgun at 1am in Delmege Park, Moyross. It was a sickening day and night in Limerick. For hours after the murder, the Campion family received phone calls and text messages from the McCarthy/Dundons, taunting them about the murder.

Nephew of the murdered man, twenty-year-old John Campion was now the only grown male belonging to the family who was not dead or locked up. Until the day his uncle was shot dead in the street, John had never come under the radar of the gardaí before. With his uncle slain and fearing further attacks on his family, John armed himself with a Smith and Wesson handgun and five rounds of .38 bullets. An X had been carved into the top of each of the bullets, which meant it would give far greater spread upon impact and cause more severe damage to the victim. Gardaí recovered the gun and ammunition underneath a coal bag in the garden of a house opposite John Campion's home. When questioned he told detectives, he got the gun for self protection shortly after his uncle was killed. John had his bail application rejected and missed his uncle's funeral. In December 2007, he was sentenced to three years' imprisonment for unlawful possession of the firearm and ammunition.

John Campion was a perfect example of how young men, who were never involved in crime in their lives, could have their future thrown into disarray when they became inescapably sucked into the world of the city's vicious criminals. In 2004, he along with his school mates went on a trip to Brussels where they were the guests of the President of the European Parliament, Pat Cox. John and his friends were brought to the top floor of the parliament buildings where they had lunch with the President and received special treatment normally reserved for visiting heads of states. John Campion had never been in trouble in his life until the day his uncle was murdered, a violent act which sparked a chain of events and ultimately led to his imprisonment.

Over, the June bank holiday weekend in 2007, a pipe bomb and balaclavas were found at the rear of a house in Pineview Gardens. The bomb disposal team had to travel to

Limerick to make the device safe. Two members of the Keane gang, one who was hiding in the attic of a nearby home, were arrested in connection with the find, but no charges were ever brought against them. Arson attacks continued on homes in Moyross and, in one week, six houses were firebombed, including that belonging to the family of murdered Aidan Kelly. On June 23, another two pipe bombs were found in Emly on the Limerick-Tipperary border. On the same day, gardaí searched fifty-three homes in Moyross and found a sub-machine gun, a machine pistol, a telescopic rifle and ammunition. Despite the intensive Garda operation, the violence continued the same night and shots were fired at a Pineview Gardens' home, while in another incident, the childhood home of feud victim Noel Campion was petrol-bombed.

In an unusual event, two horses belonging to the Keane gang were stolen by their rivals, the McCarthy/Dundons. The owners of the horses were taunted about the missing animals. Two days after they disappeared, the two missing horses were returned unharmed to the Keanes.

In some of Limerick's older estates, despite the city council's laws, horses are kept locally in green areas and back gardens. Residents in Southill, St Mary's Park and Moyross say there is a thriving 'horse culture' in their neighbourhoods where 'jocking horses (horse riding)' is seen as a good pastime to keep youths out of trouble. Adorning the gates and entrances to many homes in the same estates are decorative concrete pillars of horses. Horses used for sulky races are traded and sold for large sums of money across the city. While studying CCTV footage taken from Moyross during a criminal investigation, to their amazement, investigating officers observed a horse stabled inside a house during a late-night party. At the funeral of Noel Campion in April, his horse 'Roller' led the funeral cortege across the city to the cemetery.

Also in June 2007, twenty-three-year-old Christopher McCarthy, brother of Anthony 'Noddy' McCarthy who was convicted of the murder of Kieran Keane, was jailed for two years for couriering ammunition. Christopher McCarthy from Ballinacurra Weston pleaded guilty to unlawful possession of five rounds of 9mm Luger ammunition without a license at Childers' Road on August 29, 2006. Christopher McCarthy was arrested after a high-speed chase from O'Malley Park onto Childers' Road.

The following month in a unique case, Paul Crawford was ordered to stay away from his parents' home in O'Malley Park, after it was alleged in court that he had set up a headquarters for a major criminal gang there. Limerick City Council applied for the exclusion order against Crawford when it was claimed in the local district court that he had broken two temporary exclusion orders. Detective Sergeant Denis Treacy told the court that Crawford was a key member of the gang which were involved in the sale, supply and distribution of drugs and had been feuding with a rival city gang for a number of years, resulting in the loss of six lives over the previous eighteen months. The court heard that automatic pistols, sub-machine guns, sniper rifles, grenades and under-car explosive devices have been used by both sides in the execution of the feud.

Superintendent Frank O'Brien from Roxboro Garda station said the application being made was necessary as, 'The Southill community is greatly impacted by the presence of Paul Crawford. He is the catalyst. His life is as valuable to us as everyone else, but advice we have given to the Crawford family has been ignored.'

Judge Tom O'Donnell granted the local authority's application and ordered Crawford to stay away from the Southill estates of O'Malley Park, Keyes Park, John Carew Park and Kincora Park for eighteen months. The following month, Crawford was jailed for two years after he breached the exclusion order on three separate occasions in July and August.

In March 2008, Paul's sister, twenty-eight-year-old Mary Crawford and her friend, twenty-five-year-old Pamela Hedderman, both from Southill, were jailed for five years each when they were caught with cocaine, worth just over €275,000, hidden in a child's buggy in Colbert train station in the city on November 23, 2005. In her statement to gardaí, Mary Crawford said her brother Paul had given them €400 to go to Dublin to collect the drugs.

Also in July 2007, forty-six-year-old Stephen Fitzgerald of Island View Terrace, St Mary's Park was arrested outside the Crawford's home for threatening to kill Paul's father, John Crawford. Fitzgerald, an associate of the Keanes screamed at the Crawfords that he had shot their son, Noel, the previous December. In October 2007, he was jailed for four months for the threats outside the O'Malley Park home. It was not the last time Fitzgerald would be before the courts for a serious offence.

On July 25, the five murderers of Kieran Keane were in the Court of Criminal Appeal in Dublin, hoping to have their life convictions overturned. Their supporters in Limerick were confident that their appeals would be successful and had made preparations for a major party and massive bonfire to celebrate their release.

However, the three presiding judges had different ideas and dismissed the appeal. Pandemonium ensued as the five convicts reacted angrily, and two heavy copies of the hundred-and-five-page judgement and rosary beads were flung at the judges by two of the murderers. Solicitors were spat at and supporters of the five men hurled abuse at the legal professionals and media members in the courtroom. State solicitor in Limerick Michael Murray welcomed the Court of Criminal Appeal's rejection, saying, 'It is a very significant result and vindicates the good police work of the gardaí in Limerick who headed the investigation. I hope it will go down to those involved in the feud that the long arm of the law will eventually prevail, and that they will realise the futility of pursuing the violent agenda.'

That night armed gardaí carefully patrolled the streets of Limerick, fearing further fallout from the rejection of the appeal. Less than twenty-four-hours after the appeal was rejected, Liam Keane was arrested for being drunk and disorderly and using threatening or abusive behaviour in Limerick. It was claimed in Newport District Court that Keane went on a drinking spree, to celebrate the decision by the Court of Criminal Appeal to reject the appeals. Keane was sentenced to three months' imprisonment.

On September 2, Liam Keane stole Philip Collopy's high-powered, 2007-registered Audi A4 from outside his home in St Mary's Park. Keane was at a party in Collopy's house and stole the car keys from Philip's bedroom, before driving to a sulky rally in Roscrea, County Tipperary and on to Dublin, where the vehicle was later found crashed and burnt-out on Casement Road in Finglas. Keane, who had become a heroin addict by the time he was sentenced that November, admitted stealing the car, but denied crashing it or setting it on fire and was jailed for ten months.

As well as the main criminal feud in the city, pressurised gardaí had to contend with localised family feuds which sparked off in the Southill and Moyross areas. The Southill feud spiralled out of control and resulted in fifteen shooting incidents, eight people arrested and numerous court appearances. From the end of July, the feud between the two sides escalated and two men were shot in separate incidents.

The Southill feud took a far more sinister turn on August 19, when four shots from a high velocity rifle were fired at two plain-clothes officers in an unmarked patrol car between the estates of O'Malley Park and Keyes Park. The gunman lay in hiding and opened fire at the gardaí when they were fifty yards away with one bullet hitting the vehicle's bumper. In response, more than fifty gardaí, supported by armed detectives, the air-support unit and the Garda dog unit, searched forty properties in the Southill area, including mobile homes and sheds. Four firearms – a Glock handgun, a Beretta pistol, a rifle and a sawn-off shotgun – were seized, along with ammunition and €5,000 worth of cannabis.

Chief Superintendent Willie Keane said that the figures for illegal discharge of firearms in the first eight months of 2007 were similar to that of 2006 when 25 per cent of the entire shootings in the State took place in Limerick. 'There is a proliferation of firearms here and the amount of firearms recovered by the gardaí, and the amount of shootings, is testament to this.' Chief Supt Keane said.

Eventually, gardaí stationed at Roxboro Road intervened in the new feud and held a private meeting between the two Southill families to prevent any further incidents. Both sides agreed to a truce, but gardaí said the pact would not hinder or interfere with criminal prosecutions and investigations. Superintendent Frank O'Brien said the serious consequences of the ongoing feud were pointed out to the two sides during the meeting. The Garda intervention worked and following that there was no further trouble between the two families.

While the talk amongst the city's politicians was 'regeneration' and the hope of a new beginning for Limerick's troubled suburbs, in St Mary's Park and the greater King's Island area the shootings and violence continued. Over the course of a fortnight, there were six shootings in the area. Nineteen-year-old Ian Brennan of Westbury, Corbally, County Clare, was shot twice by an assailant armed with a shotgun in St Munchin's Street, St Mary's Park on

September 23, following a row in nearby pub.

On September 25, a gunman fired a shot through the front door of a home in Assumpta Park, Island Road. On the night of October 2/3, a spate of shootings took place across the city. Four gunshots were fired into a home in Richmond Estate in Corbally at 10.30pm. A few hours later, a number of shots were fired at a man's home in Glencairn, Dooradoyle. The occupant of the home was in serious drugs debt to one of the gangs.

Back in St Mary's Park, a Limerick gang left their calling cards at two houses after the occupants had fallen behind in loan repayments to the outfit. At 2.05am, a woman, who was sleeping in the sitting room of her family home in St Munchin's Street, was awoken by the sound of gunfire as two shots hit her front door. While gardaí investigated the scene, a brazen assailant opened fire on another family on the same street, at 4.50am, with four gunshots hitting the house. The gang had taken over a money-lending racket, and vulnerable people who could not get loans from financial institutions turned to the gang for assistance. Upon granting a loan, the gang took possession of all of the social welfare child-benefit books in the family's possession and used these for the debt repayments. All books were held onto until the loan, including hefty interest rates, was repaid. A pump-action shotgun was used in the four shootings.

On October 6, at 12.30am, a family had a lucky escape when seven shots were fired into their home in St Mary's Park and at, 5.30am, on the same morning two shots were fired at an Assumpta Park home. Such were the frequency of shootings in the St Mary's Park area, it was only a matter of time before another life was claimed by the gangs and the latest atrocity in the city duly arrived on the night of October 8.

That night Gareth Grant was shot dead as he walked near his home in the St Mary's Park estate. Gardaí arrived quickly on the scene but were unable to revive him. A man was charged with his murder in January 2009.

The week after the cold-blooded murder, senior gardaí in the city addressed the City Council's Joint Policing Committee and gave a broad view of what they were working at on both sides of the city and the obstacles they faced. Detective Superintendent Jim Browne told the gathering that gardaí were investigating the activities of twelve individuals who were pressurising younger people to carry out their drugs deals and arson attacks on homes. The city council hoped to bring further exclusion orders against these culprits who were causing havoc across the estates of Southill, Moyross, St Mary's Park and Ballinacurra Weston. Those at the meeting also heard that, of the fifty firearms recovered in the city for the ten months of 2007, the majority of firearms seized originated from Eastern Europe. In 2006, seventy illegally-held guns were seized by officers.

Before October had ended, there was further trouble in Moyross and brothers, twenty-seven-year-old Philip and forty-one-year-old Ray 'Jethro' Collopy were arrested for threatening to kill a married man, Michael Cleary, on October 30, 2007.

Ray 'Jethro' Collopy, with an address in St Patrick's Avenue, Limerick, was a father-of-three and a European champion pike fisherman. Ray Collopy got a taxi into Moyross on the night in question and met his brother Philip Collopy from St Munchin's Street who was wearing a bullet-proof vest. The two brothers went to the Cleary house in Sarsfield Gardens where they were met by a female relative of Michael Cleary's. She saw the Collopy brothers and another man standing outside. Philip Collopy roared up at her, 'Tell Michael he's going to get a 45 (.45-calibre fire-arm).' While saying this, he made a gun gesture and pointed at his head.

When Michael Cleary went outside the home he was approached by Ray Collopy who was urged on by his brother, Philip, 'Go on, go up and shoot him.'

At their sentencing, defence solicitor Ted McCarthy said the two brothers had been at a funeral of an elderly neighbour in St Mary's Park earlier that day and had been drinking, 'to such an extent that they were a danger to themselves'. They each received suspended sentences of sixteen months' imprisonment for making the threats, and the pair was also ordered to be of good behaviour for a period of two years and to stay out of Moyross for the same time.

Across the city in Southill, a nineteen-year-old son was taken from his parents when he was brutally murdered just yards from his home. Jeffrey Hannan was last seen at a bon-fire near his home at Galtee Drive, O'Malley Park, by his mother, Geraldine around 2am on November 22. This was the last time her son would be seen alive. He had gone out shortly before midnight after a few friends called around to him to drink a few cans. The following morning, Jeffrey's body was found less than a hundred yards from his terraced home. He had been beaten around the head with a blunt object and died from severe head injuries. The young Limerick man had just returned home from Manchester and was hoping to begin work as a trainee barman. He celebrated the first birthday of his daughter a fortnight before he was murdered. Jeffrey used to accompany his father, Alan, to Limerick hurling matches.

'He was a lovely fella with a one-year-old child. He gave her a bike for her birthday. He had a great time with his daughter and a lovely party. She is the image of him,' his devastated father said.

Unable to look at the spot where their son was killed, the Hannan family left Southill shortly afterwards and moved to a new home in the city, but the grief of their son's murder stays with them every day. Southill is at the heart of the government's regeneration plan for the city's southside, but for families like the Hannans it arrived too late. At the time of going to press, the investigation into the killing of Jeffrey Hannan is ongoing.

13

Arms Plot Foiled

In the visiting area of Wheatfield Prison in Dublin, twenty-seven-year-old John Dundon looked at the newspaper left in front of him. He nodded in acknowledgement at the visitor, who was wearing an 'Old Navy' T-shirt in the adjacent cubicle and speaking to a convict from Dublin.

It was April 5, 2007 and contained within the paper left with the Limerick man were the contact details for the major arms dealer sitting near him. The dealer's name was also 'John'.

Less than two months before the Wheatfield prison encounter, a front man acting on behalf of the Dundons had held initial discussions with the gun dealer and his colleague in a London warehouse, concerning a lucrative proposition to import a lethal haul of sophisticated weaponry to Ireland. The McCarthy/Dundon gang was convinced that the second secret meeting, within the confines of one the country's most secure prisons, would give them the upper hand in Limerick's criminal feud and provide them with the opportunity to finally wipe out the leadership of the rival Keane/Collopy gangs in an ultimate vicious settling of the city's blood feud.

The gang believed that the British arms dealer could provide them with an arsenal of weapons – enough to equip a small military unit. Following the prison meeting, the gang soon decided on what military hardware they wanted to import to the country and provided the dealers with their lengthy shopping list: two Russian-designed RPG-7 grenade launchers, five Russian AKM 7.62mm assault rifles, five AR-15 assault rifles, two Uzi sub-machine guns, three Smith & Wesson 9mm semi-automatics, two Browning 9mm semi-automatics and five SIG-Sauer 9mm semi-automatics, along with over 200 rounds of ammunition of .23-inch bullets and .762 bullets. It was a terrifying inventory capable of inflicting untold damage.

The arms importation plot was hatched, directed and co-ordinated by the gang's leadership from inside the high-security Dublin prison.

But the man dressed in the 'Old-Navy' T-shirt in Wheatfield Prison wasn't the underworld arms dealer he was posing as. In fact, unknown to John Dundon, he was sitting across from a highly trained undercover officer from Britain's elite Special Organised Crime Agency (SOCA). Fears of a major escalation in the vicious Limerick gang feud and Garda intelligence led senior officers, authorised by Assistant Commissioner Nacie Rice, to enlist the help of the special British unit and the agent's presence in Wheatfield Prison was an elaborate part of a sting operation by the gardaí as their investigations into the McCarthy/Dundon gangs' activities intensified. The Crime and Security Branch at Garda HQ worked with the SOCA to use two undercover British agents to pose as arms dealers after they learned that the McCarthy/Dundons were 'shopping' for high-powered weapons as part of the city's vicious feud. SOCA was created, on April 1, 2006, through the merger of four major British judicial agencies. The agency's role was to address serious and organised crime in the UK, and covert missions are undertaken by highly trained police officers under strict regulatory controls. These missions range from dealing with firearms, drug-trafficking, money-laundering and crimes that potentially put human life at risk. Trained undercover operatives named 'John' and 'Raj' worked with gardaí in the major arms conspiracy operation. The real identities of the SOCA officers were protected throughout and at the subsequent court case.

Twenty-seven-year-old Glen Geasley from Innishmore Drive, Ballincollig, County Cork, and twenty-one-year-old Seán Callinan of Pearse Park, Tullamore, County Offaly, were used as pawns by the gang to purchase the arms. On February 22, 2007, Geasley was met by another SOCA agent, named George, in London who brought him to meet the two undercover SOCA agents in an old Victorian warehouse underneath a railway arch. Geasley was authorised by the Dundons to purchase the arsenal of weapons for them and, not surprisingly, the initial meeting in London was a tense affair and both sides exercised extreme caution. Both the arms dealers/British agents and Geasley took off their outer clothes, to demonstrate that they were not wired or armed. Unknown to the Corkman, the warehouse had already been rigged by SOCA, and the entire first meeting between the arms buyers and the British agents was recorded.

Geasley told the fake arms dealers that he was representing a man called Wayne Dundon and was acting on his behalf. The two agents were later told that Dundon was 'the decision man' and that, '[They] needed all the weapons for a war in Limerick between Wayne's [Dundon] people and their enemies.'

Geasley was shown an array of weapons on a laptop computer and provided with a price list for various munitions which the arms dealers could supply and he left the warehouse with mobile phone contact numbers. However, the SOCA agents, who were liaising with the gardaí, were moving with extreme care and informed Geasley that they wanted to establish that he was acting for precisely who he claimed he was.

Incredibly, a meeting was arranged for one of the arms dealers/agents to meet criminal, John Dundon, Wayne's brother, inside Wheatfield Prison in Dublin. The cloak-and-dagger meeting involved the arms dealer/agent 'John' visiting another inmate, Thomas Flood, on April 5, 2007. In the prisoner's cubicle, right beside the arms dealer/SOCA agent was John Dundon. The arms dealer/agent brought a copy of the *Irish Independent* with him, inside which on pages 15/16, was an insertion from a British magazine, *London Life*. The agent had replaced two pages of the *Irish Independent* with pages of the British magazine which contained an ad for mobile phones. The mobile number of the ad was the contact number for 'John' for further talks about the proposed shipment of weapons. The newspaper and insert was left beside John Dundon who took it away. The agent was also asked to wear a branded T-shirt and this brand, 'Old Navy', then became their identification code-word for future contact. As John Dundon got up, he nodded in acknowledgement to the undercover agent. There had been no other communication between them. As far as Dundon was concerned, it was a carefully orchestrated and covert meeting. The meeting in the prison was also recorded. Within days, the fake arms dealers were contacted with a detailed shopping list of weapons which they agreed to sell for St£45,000 or €59,700. The money was to be paid in cash, a date for collection was agreed, and the transaction was to take place in Cork.

On April 20, Agent 'Raj' rang Glen Geasley to say he was at Rochestown Park Hotel, on the southside of Cork City and wanted the cash, before the arms shipment could be handed over. In the subsequent court case, the State alleged that Dessie Dundon was contacted in prison via mobile phone and he demanded two sample weapons, before the cash was handed over, for the purpose of test firing. However, Raj insisted that this was impossible and offered the compromise of a photograph taken on his mobile-phone camera. Geasley was shown a photograph of the rocket-propelled grenade launcher and a copy of that day's *Evening Herald* newspaper to verify the consignment. Raj then demanded payment up front of the full St£45,000 for the entire shipment and Geasley handed over the cash in used British and Northern Ireland bank notes in a Tommy Hilfiger sports bag.

The SOCA agent, 'John' was at the Ibis Hotel in Dunkettle on the outskirts of Cork City with the weapons consignment and Seán Callinan was told where to meet him. The firearms cache was made up of weapons seized by the gardaí from paramilitaries during the northern troubles. Armed officers closely monitored the parked van containing the arms from nearby vantage points. Callinan approached agent 'John' and was brought to the van and shown the weapons. Immediately, gardaí pounced on their targets. Callinan was surrounded by members of the ERU and arrested as was Geasley at the Rochestown Park Hotel, and the bag of St£45,000 was seized. In Wheatfield prison, the cells of the Dundons were searched and three mobile phones were found along with the London magazine insertion brought to the meeting in the visiting area. In a search of Geasley's apartment, a hardback book called *Small Arms* was found. The Dundons were left reeling by the success of the covert Garda operation.

Geasley and Callinan were both convicted criminals before they attempted to buy the arsenal of weapons. Geasley had thirteen previous convictions while Callinan had seventeen previous convictions. The two were charged, held in custody and were eventually tried in Cork Circuit Criminal Court, in February 2008, where they were each charged with four similar but separate offences relating to the firearms conspiracy between February 22 and April 20. Both pleaded not guilty to the charges. When the details of the sinister plot were revealed in 2008, it became all too clear to the country, the lengths to which the McCarthy/Dundon gang would go to inflict carnage on their enemies.

Opening the State's case, Tom O'Connell SC, said the jury would be presented with video recordings and audio tapes of meetings between the SOCA agents and various parties in relation to the alleged arms conspiracy. When agent 'John' was sworn in to give evidence, he was visible to both the accused, the jury, both legal teams and Judge Patrick Moran, but was shielded from the public in courtroom two at the Washington Street Courthouse. Mr O'Connell told the jury that for security reasons it was necessary to screen 'John' and 'Raj' from the public gallery, so that their identities could not be disclosed.

However, following successive days of legal argument the trial ended dramatically on the eleventh day, on February 25, when Geasley and Callinan asked to be re-arraigned and pleaded guilty to a single charge of conspiring with others to procure the arsenal of weapons. The about-turn came after Judge Moran ruled in favour of the prosecution that covert video and audio recordings were admissible as evidence.

Detective Chief Superintendent Tony Quilter told the

court that Geasley was acting under the direction and influence of others and said that Callinan 'got in over his head'.

It was a massive victory for the State and Geasley was
jailed for twelve years, with five years suspended, while
Callinan was jailed for six years, with three years suspended. Geasley had his sentence backdated to April 20,
2007 when he was first taken into custody. However, Callinan committed the arms conspiracy offence while out on
bail and did not commence his jail term until October 23,
2008 when he had completed his previous sentence. The
gravity of the offences did not go unnoticed by Judge
Moran who when passing sentence warned that the consequences of such an arms shipment reaching its intended
target would have been 'very serious for the people of this
country'.

It was a landmark case, and it hadn't escaped anyone's
attention that Limerick's vicious gang feud had spread from
within the confines of an Irish prison to the shady world of
European arms dealers. For the first time, undercover
agents from a European police force had been recruited for
a joint operation aimed at foiling attempts by an Irish organised crime gang to secure heavy weaponry. Crucially, these
agents were also empowered to operate within Ireland. The
arms conspiracy resembled an international espionage
operation – combining undercover agents, codenames,
micro-TV bugging, military-style weaponry, carefully
orchestrated prison meetings, secret identities and designer
bags stuffed with money.

Former Soviet-block weaponry remains readily available

in parts of Eastern Europe, but with European security forces on high alert over the threat posed by Islamic terrorists, getting such weapons in the UK and Ireland remains problematic. Detectives suspect that the McCarthy/Dundons were determined to obtain Russian-made Kalashnikov RPG-7 grenade launchers for two reasons: It would offer them a dramatic firepower advantage over their gang enemies and it would also facilitate a series of spectacular, targeted assassinations.

The Kalashnikov RPG-7 rocket-propelled grenade launcher was designed by the Red Army in the 1960s to dramatically improve the firepower available to infantry soldiers and is capable of hitting targets at up to 500 metres in range. The RPG-7 is normally used with a 2.6kg warhead and reached the IRA's arsenal via shipments from Libya where it remained in devastating use for twenty years. The RPG warhead can penetrate up to 30cm of lightly armoured targets, and if used against vehicles like unprotected army or police cars or prison escorts can inflict horrific damage.

The outcome of the arms conspiracy was clear to all. The Limerick feud would continue and was being directed by some of the most senior members of the gangs who were clearly intent on seeing it out to the bitter end, despite the fact they were locked up behind bars serving lengthy sentences. The State's most powerful act against any law breaker lies in its ability to deprive criminals of their liberty. It was becoming obvious, that this power alone was not enough to deal with Limerick's problems.

14

Innocent Men Die

President Mary McAleese visited Moyross and Southill in early 2008, and it marked the opportunity of a new beginning for the neighbourhoods. Real, tangible hope arose, and all fervently wished that the dark days were consigned to the past.

But 2008 began violently. On January 7, at 11.30pm, the widow of murdered Kieran Keane, Sophie, and her seventeen-year-old son, Kieran, were shot at while in their home in Garryowen. The mother and son were lucky to escape unharmed.

Less than a fortnight into the New Year and gun crime, which had previously been largely confined to the city's troubled enclaves, was brought into the city centre. On the evening of January 11, the city was full of Friday rush-hour traffic when eighteen-year-old Jonathan Fitzgerald was shot at in Parnell Street in front of shocked motorists and pedestrians. The young Limerick man was shot in the neck and leg by a gunman who hid his identity with a balaclava. A bullet also ripped through the jacket of his companion, who was standing alongside him. Rapidly losing blood, the teenage victim struggled to make his escape in the direction of Wickham Street but collapsed on the ground while the man responsible fled in a Toyota in the direction of Hyde Road.

Despite having their suspicions, there was insufficient evidence for the gardaí to prosecute.

Jonathan's father, Stephen Fitzgerald was sentenced to four months' imprisonment for threatening the Crawfords in Southill in 2007. His son, Jonathan, the target in January 2008, had been arrested shortly after a murder in 2006, but was never charged in connection with it. After the Parnell-Street shooting, Jonathan Fitzgerald was kept on a life-support machine in the Mid-Western Regional Hospital, and survived.

An alarming phenomenon occurring in Limerick was the increased use of teenagers, children and young vulnerable people by criminal gangs for their activities.

The weekend before President McAleese arrived in Limerick, twenty residents in King's Island contacted Labour TD Jan O'Sullivan, requesting they be moved from their local-authority housing, following four gun attacks on homes in St Mary's Park. The shootings took place on January 18/19 and, in one incident, the home of a pensioner was shot at for the second time in three months. Another attack took place when a gunman opened fire on a house in St

Ita's Street, while gardaí were at the scene of a shooting on St Munchin's Street. Two youths were arrested and questioned; one was aged nineteen, the other was thirteen years old. The gangs were using boys as young as ten to carry out nefarious dealings for them, including: attacking homes and property, drug dealing, antisocial behaviour and hiding contraband such as narcotics and high-powered weapons. Evidence of this came before the courts in 2008.

In March, the city's juvenile court heard that a fifteen-year-old school boy was warned that his head would be blown off and his family threatened, if he did not hide a loaded Magnum handgun for the McCarthy/Dundon gang. The youth was charged with possession of the gun and three rounds of ammunition. Ballistics tests showed that the gun had been used in previous gangland shootings and was found by officers in a garden shed at the rear of a house at Hyde Road, Ballinacurra Weston. The youth avoided a jail sentence, following an impressive probation report.

Responding to the case at the time, Superintendent Frank O'Brien said, 'Unscrupulous individuals at the high end of feud-related activity are targeting children and grooming them. These are vulnerable young people who believe this criminality gives them status as hard men.'

Further evidence of vulnerable young men targeted by gangs came in the case of eighteen-year-old Robert Corbett from Crecora Avenue, Ballinacurra Weston. Cannabis worth €5,000 was recovered from a shed at the back of his home on May 3, 2008. Limerick District Court heard that the gang had selected Corbett as he was an easy target. He had been promised money and street cred in return for storing the cannabis. Corbett suffered from attention deficit hyperactivity disorder (ADHD), had no formal second-level education and was preyed upon after his father went into hospital. When gardaí recovered the drugs, the Corbett family were threatened and had to repay the dealers twice the value of the outstanding drugs debt. If the gangs were not refunded for their loss by the individual they held responsible, then family members or their homes were targeted.

When Robert Corbett's case came to court, Detective David Nolan of Roxboro Garda station told Judge Tom O'Donnell that this kind of situation happens on a regular basis in Limerick. Robert Corbett pleaded guilty to possession of the cannabis with intent to sell or supply, but avoided a jail sentence and was ordered to remain under the supervision of the probation services for a year.

One of the most shocking cases of teenagers involved in gangland activity arose in the early hours of April 2. A fourteen-year-old boy was arrested at 1.30am for driving a car in St Mary's Park while wearing a bulletproof vest and carrying a knife. He was brought to Henry Street Garda station and released into the custody of an adult a short time later. However, the youth was about to get himself into further trouble. He smoked weed and cannabis and drank cans of Budweiser before meeting up with nineteen-year-old Michael Ryan from St Munchin's Street, St Mary's Park. The pair, armed with a double-barrel, sawn-off shotgun, went to a house in St Munchin's Street and the fourteen-year-old opened fire twice on the property at 6.15am.

Shotgun pellets hit the front door and the family car, before the youth was overheard saying to Ryan, 'the gun jammed sham'. The pair fled from the scene on foot and were both later found by investigating gardaí asleep in the top bunk in a bedroom of Ryan's home. The firearm, which had been stolen from the Rathkeale area in 2005, was recovered nearby. Both the youth and Ryan made admissions to gardaí.

The fourteen-year-old told Detective Gerard Cleary that he shot at the house, because he felt like it. He openly told officers he pulled the trigger of the shotgun as 'I usually shoot with my left hand.' Probation reports showed that the fourteen-year-old associated with criminals in St Mary's Park, while Ryan was influenced by a local gang, and the two had little parental control.

When the case came to court, both defendants pleaded guilty to: possession of a double-barrel, sawn-off shotgun and three twelve-gage shotgun cartridges in suspicious circumstances, damage to a 2006-registered car and damage to the front door of the home at St Munchin's Street. The fourteen-year-old was prosecuted under the Children's Act and, in October 2008, Judge Carroll Moran imposed a detention and supervisory order totalling five years.

Although Ryan did not fire the gun, Judge Carroll Moran said he 'must take considerable responsibility and culpability for what happened' and jailed him for four years.

In mid-March in an interview with the *Irish Independent*, Limerick State solicitor Michael Murray issued a warning that a small group of godfathers continued to remain

untouchable because of a ready supply of willing lieutenants to fill any void created by the successful prosecution
and jailing of their predecessors. Michael Murray described
the activities of those controlling Limerick's drugs scene and
the city's gangs as 'unrelenting'.

The feud was about to hit the headlines once again. On
the evening of March 25, a silver-coloured, Dublin-registered Mercedes, with a taxi plate on the roof, entered St
Mary's Park at 8.45pm. At the time, children were playing
on the streets with the schools closed for Easter holidays.
Nobody paid much heed to the taxi or its occupants as it
slowly made its way down to St Ita's Street – home to members of the Collopy family and their associates. Suddenly
the taxi speeded up and a man armed with an automatic
sub-machine gun emerged from the passenger window and
opened fire. Bullets were sprayed at six homes alongside
each other. One woman walking on the street narrowly
escaped injury as families with young children dived for
cover indoors. Miraculously nobody was killed in the hail of
fire.

It was a cunning and devious attack by the
McCarthy/Dundons on their sworn enemies. The
high-powered Mercedes had been stolen in Rathfarnham,
Dublin, on St Patrick's Day, before it was brought to Limerick to be used in the attack. It was fitted with a taxi plate,
and the gang had a getaway black Toyota Corolla standing
by at the Cronan Grove estate, Shannon, County Clare.

A large public outcry followed. Chairman of Limerick's
Joint Policing Committee and Fine Gael councillor Kevin

Kiely called on Justice Minister Brian Lenihan to introduce emergency legislation to allow for the immediate internment of known criminal figures. Kevin Kiely argued that, 'The Minister should move immediately to introduce emergency legislation to protect innocent people before someone is killed.' Such laws could allow a Chief Superintendent swear an affidavit against people who are members of criminal gangs and have easy access to firearms.

Two days after the gun attack, Justice Minister Brian Lenihan and Garda Commissioner Fachtna Murphy were in Limerick and met with senior gardaí to receive an update on the city's feuding criminal gangs and they visited the estates of Moyross and Southill. The Emergency Response Unit (ERU) was ordered to return to patrol the troubled estates after Justice Minister Brian Lenihan said the situation could explode at any minute. The ERU had been used by senior gardaí at intervening periods throughout the years. They were deployed following gangland murders or when officers feared the feud was about to erupt in further bloodshed.

The ERU had only been patrolling the flashpoint areas for just over a week when two murders brought the city to another low. On the afternoon of April 5, residents across Limerick were settling down in front of their TVs for an afternoon's sporting entertainment. Two particular events taking place in England were to be the day's highlights as thousands from the city had travelled to Gloucester for Munster's Heineken Cup quarter-final match against the English club, while the bookies were also full with anxious punters wagering bets on that day's Aintree Grand National.

On the same day Mark Maloney was shot and died as he walked through this home neighbourhood of Garryowen.

Less than forty-eight hours after Moloney's death, gardaí were searching for evidence in open ground near Caledonian Park when they made a horrific discovery – the body of James Cronin buried in a shallow grave. Cronin had been lured to the area and shot in the head. Two firearms and ammunition were also found.

Limerick was in shock at the violent deaths. A black week followed with the attention of the nation once again firmly fixed on the city's feuding factions.

Chief Superintendent Willie Keane appealed through the author in the *Irish Independent* to those involved in the feud to take stock of the situation: 'Where is it getting them, it is resulting in death, serious injury or disability. It is resulting in long terms of imprisonment and sadness and bereavement for families here. So it is pain all the way through; there are just no winners.

'The feuding in Limerick, some commentators have put it down to drugs and turf wars. That element is there, but it is deeper than that in Limerick unfortunately. It is into hatred and family hatred and this overwhelming desire to seek vengeance and of course, when something happens, there is this immediate need to get vengeance.

'I am very concerned. There are fifty-five people in custody at the moment that we would directly link to the feuding families, so that is a huge number and that is just directly linked to the primary families. Unfortunately, there are people that are too willing to take their place. That is the sad aspect of it.'

The night before James Cronin's funeral, brother-in-law of murdered Mark Moloney, and a relative of Robert Fitzgerald, who was shot dead in 2003, forty-six-year-old Stephen Fitzgerald was arrested with a parabellum Glock semi-automatic pistol and two magazines with nineteen rounds of 9mm Luger ammunition at the Canal Bank in Rhebogue. Originally from Island View Terrace, St Mary's Park, Fitzgerald had the honour of becoming the first man in the State to have a taser gun used to stun him by arresting officers. He pleaded guilty to unlawful possession of the weapon and ammunition and was sentenced in March 2009 to four years' imprisonment. At his sentencing, Detective Cathal O'Neill said Fitzgerald was a 'fully integrated member of the Keane/Collopy criminal gang', a claim Fitzgerald denied.

Bishop of Limerick, Donal Murray, who made appeals in the past, only for them to be later ignored, said that the violence was 'the tragic fruit of greed, hatred and the desire for revenge'.

At Cronin's funeral mass, Fr John Dunworth spoke of how the city had evolved through the ages, but warned that people living in twenty-first-century Limerick must remain on the alert to the dangers that lurks near their home:

'Limerick City is one of Ireland's oldest cities dating back over a thousand years. It used to be a walled in city to protect its citizens. Parts of the city are called after the gates through the old walls: Watergate, Thomondgate; the ruins of those walls are still seen today. In ancient times, the walls were manned by watchmen and if an enemy approached, they shouted "enemy approaching" to alert its citizens. Sadly today, the trouble lies within the city, but the citizens still need to be on the alert, danger is around us.'

Before the month was out, another man had been shot, but managed to survive. On the afternoon of April 23, McCarthy/Dundon gang member, forty-one-year-old Jimmy Collins, was walking near his home in Hyde Avenue in Ballinacurra Weston when he was shot twice in a drive-by shooting by of the Keane gang. Up to fourteen bullets were fired at Collins, and the culprits escaped in the green Honda Prelude car which was later found burnt-out. Collins has tattoos of handguns and ones which commemorate 'Fat Frankie' Ryan on his chest. He always wore a bulletproof vest and escaped from the daylight gun attack with wounds to his leg. The Glock semi-automatic pistol used to shoot Collins was recovered less than a fortnight later when a stolen, silver Mazda RX 80 sports car, being driven by twenty-three-year-old Liam Keane, was forced off the road by members of the ERU at Athlunkard Road, Corbally, County Clare. The firearm was found in the foot well of the vehicle and was cocked and ready for use. Officers arrested Liam Keane and another man. Both men were held in custody while waiting for their case to come before the courts.

At this stage, Liam Keane has amassed up to fifty criminal convictions, despite his young age. The majority of offences committed were for road-traffic offences, but he became one of the country's best-known gang members, following his two-fingered reaction to press photographers when he walked free from the Eric Leamy murder trial. During his young life, he received a variety of convictions and was in and out of prison, where he became a heroin addict.

When he was arrested in Corbally in May 2008, Keane had only just been released from prison, on April 18, having served a ten-month sentence for stealing Philip Collopy's Audi A4 from outside his home in St Mary's Park in September 2007. Philip was the leader of the Collopy gang and Keane's neighbour, and was pitted against the McCarthy/Dundons.

Even while locked up in Limerick Prison, Liam Keane, whose appearance began to bear the signs of heroin abuse, managed to get in trouble after he used a Nokia mobile phone to send images of himself to his girlfriend who uploaded them onto a Bebo website. His phone was discovered by prison authorities in his cell in July and, as punishment, Keane was barred from visits, phone calls and recreational time in the jail for a month.

In the Circuit Criminal Court, Liam Keane and the other young man pleaded guilty to unlawful possession of the Glock semi-automatic pistol and thirteen rounds of 9mm ammunition. Ballistics tests showed the gun was the same weapon used in the attack on Jimmy Collins, but nobody was ever charged for the shooting.

When interviewed by gardaí, Keane rejected suggestions that he was going to assassinate anyone on the night he was arrested: 'I was caught in Corbally. All my enemies are on the other side of town. I wasn't going to shoot anybody.'

Keane claimed to have picked the gun up in a field 'out

the Ballysimon way' and had it because of the way his uncle, Kieran Keane, ended up. When asked why the gangs hated each other so much, he replied: 'That's life, that's the way it goes.'

In the end the courts went tough on Liam Keane, by then a father-of-one, and he was sentenced to ten years' imprisonment for the offences in January 2009. The other young man arrested with Liam Keane was also convicted and sentenced to ten years' imprisonment.

Judge Carroll Moran said, 'It seems that they were in possession of the gun for a serious, sinister purpose of an immediate nature which cannot be specified.'

Keane also received a concurrent three-year sentence, after he pleaded guilty to unauthorised possession of a 2005, Dublin-registered Mazda RX. Ironically, Liam received the sentence less than a month before his father was due to be released from prison. A week later, another six months was added to Liam Keane's ten years' sentence, after he admitted that he had hidden a Nokia mobile phone in the bunk of his prison cell.

The Criminal Assets Bureau (CAB), assisted by two Limerick-based profilers, were putting together a portfolio of the gang's assets, which they had acquired from illegal enterprise.

At the beginning of 2008, January sales of a different kind were taking place, where criminals under the intense scrutiny of the CAB raced to liquidate their assets and properties. One house in Ballinacurra Weston was offered for sale for €12,000. Houses across the city were raided and inspected, and officers photographed and listed the value of houses belonging to criminals and their entire contents. CAB profilers began trawling though accounts in banks, building societies, post offices, credit unions and even bookmakers. Just before the double murders in April, the CAB seized two vehicles, a BMW X5 4X4 and a BMW 3 series car, both worth in excess of €150,000. They were registered to brothers, Ger and Wayne Dundon. Such was the fear of further attacks, the McCarthy/Dundons were now purchasing armour-plated vehicles which they imported from Germany. The two vehicles were equipped with bulletproof, reinforced glass over an inch thick and came with armour plating meaning they could withstand an assault from an AK 47 or MI6 rifle. They were also built to survive a small-scale explosion under the chassis. Special steel and other materials, including aramid fibres (as used in bulletproof vests), were used to strengthen the exterior. The BMW X5 came equipped with a PA system and a 4.4ltr petrol engine. Young McCarthy/Dundon gang members drove around the outside of Limerick prison, taunting inmates and rival criminals inside the jail through the loud PA system.

At 6am on May 8, the CAB launched a massive offensive against the gangs with 'Operation Platinum'. It was the biggest single Garda operation against organised crime ever undertaken in the Mid-West region. Uniformed and detective units from the divisions of Limerick, Cork and Kerry, CAB officers and members of the criminal and fraud investigation bureaus and the national drugs units began entering homes at first light, while armed gardaí patrolled outside. In the preceding days, dozens of warrants to search properties had been secured, in a bid to uncover an intricate paper trail. Officers raided the offices of legal firms, accountants, auditors, a credit union and more than 120 homes in Limerick. Computers, safes, hard drives and bundles of files were seized, along with drugs, cash, firearms, ammunition and top-of-the-range vehicles by more than 250 gardaí. In Dublin, a solicitor and accountant's office was searched along with three residences in Portmarnock and Coolock. From the raids, €250,000 was seized in twelve locations. Chief Superintendent Willie Keane said the investigation was one of the biggest ever mounted in the State.

In October the CAB was granted permission by the High Court to sell a Toyota Landcruiser and a Toyota Avensis seized from the Keane/Collopy gang. The vehicles had belonged to twenty-eight-year-old Philip Collopy from St Mary's Park and twenty-eight-year-old Brian Scanlon, who was originally from Cork, but also had addresses at St Mary's Park and in Murroe, County Limerick. The legal action was based on the State's contention that the vehicles represented the proceeds of crime, and neither Collopy nor Scanlon contested the action.

One of the more surprising revelations uncovered was that a relative of the McCarthy/Dundons had invested huge sums of cash in State-sponsored prize bonds. As opposed to hiding large sums of cash which can be found, prize bonds investments are guaranteed to be returned in full. Those investing in prize bonds are also entered into weekly draws where 2,500 tax free prizes are on offer, including cash prizes, which were not liable to income tax, capital gains tax or DIRT. In one particular raid, officers found registered prize bonds worth in excess of €30,000 and paperwork relating to shares purchased in Leeds United Football Club.

Following the massive offensive launched by the gardaí, Limerick's criminals were feeling the strain of the intense scrutiny of the CAB and were finding that their movements were constantly monitored by authorities. A tentative truce was agreed between the main feuding factions in mid-May, but this was generally viewed with great scepticism due to the nature of those involved. Nevertheless shootings in the city dropped greatly over the following months and until November 2008 there were only a handful of isolated shooting incidents.

On one occasion, outside the district court, Ger Dundon – the youngest son of Kenneth Dundon – approached photographers, identified himself and declared there was no feud in Limerick. Come July, twenty-one-year-old Ger appeared before the same court under tight security and was sentenced to ten months' imprisonment for thirty-four motoring offences.

Dundon's solicitor John Devane said in Limerick District Court on July 9, 2008 that his client lived under the constant fear of being murdered: 'He is aware there is a €1m contract on his head, because of who his family are. He cannot walk the streets of Limerick City or any other city in the country. He has been given motor vehicles by his family for his own protection and has a bulletproof BMW.'

Ger Dundon was also banned from driving for fifteen years, but appealed the convictions to the Circuit Court. In August, he was sentenced to another nine months' imprisonment for possession of a false passport while trying to board a flight to Amsterdam from Cork Airport on July 4. Ger told gardaí he had the passport in the name of Terence Ruth for his own protection and was going to the Netherlands for a few days as he had been advised that his life was in danger. He was later freed temporarily after he appealed the sentences to the Circuit Court. His older brother, John Dundon, was released from prison on July 31, having served his sentence for threatening Owen Treacy and immediately returned to Limerick, where his associates held a big party to celebrate his homecoming.

The same summer, forty-eight-year-old Sean 'Cowboy' Hanley was sentenced to ten years' imprisonment after he was caught with 3kg of amphetamines in Mountrath, County Laois, on September 2, 2004. Cowboy Hanley, who had a house in Creaval Park, Moyross, was convicted alongside John Costello, who received twelve years. Costello had provided gardaí with an address at Hennessy Avenue, Kileely. He was driving the car from Dublin when it was blocked by the officers from the National Drug Unit.

After Eddie Ryan's murder in 2000, Cowboy aligned himself alongside the McCarthy/Dundons in a bid to wrestle control of the drugs trade from the Keanes and Collopys. While awaiting trial for the drugs offence, arsonists targeted a home belonging to Cowboy in Moyross in April 2007. Cowboy's son, twenty-year-old Brian Hanley was stabbed to death at Cregan Avenue, Kileely, in August 2001. At the time of his death, Brian was awaiting trial in connection with a major drugs find at Meelick, County Clare, the previous June when ecstasy worth £IR1m was recovered. The CAB was also looking into Cowboy Hanley who sold his farm for over €3m in 2004.

Hopes of an end to the feud were raised when Chief Executive of the newly set up Limerick Regeneration Agencies, Brendan Kenny, offered to talk to the city's gangs and held a series of meetings with both sides. Throughout, Brendan Kenny maintained that the meetings would not hinder ongoing Garda investigations, but argued that there had to be some form of interaction as people would, eventually, have to live together in the regenerated areas. Some saw it as the first concrete attempts towards ending the feud. Others such as Mayor of Limerick John Gilligan were outraged at the negotiations. John Gilligan said he would be 'absolutely ... horrified if we are going down the road of sitting down with these people to end the feuding without looking at the central issue which is the fact that they are poisoning the youth of our country with drugs.

'They are killing people every single day, every time they sell drugs. What they are doing is wrong. ... You can't support the fact that these people sell drugs, you have to be clear and unequivocal about that.

'Drugs in Ireland have devastated whole areas and I will not be party to anybody who will give any succour to people who are selling drugs in my city. There can be no compromise with this and I am totally ... against it.'

Despite the lull in violence, gardaí were taking no chances and at the beginning of September, their new Regional Support Units (RSU) were unveiled. The units were devised by a Garda review group following the Abbeylara stand-off in 2000 when John Carthy was fatally injured by gardaí after a confrontation at his home. Less lethal forms of force were needed to tackle serious situations. The new units, which were initially deployed to serve Limerick and Cork, were to respond to major incidents involving firearms or the taking of a hostage rather than wait for the Dublin-based ERU. The units would operate normally as unarmed, uniformed gardaí but would switch into tactical, bulletproof and protective clothing if ordered to respond to a critical incident. Purpose-built, Volvo XC 70 police specials with a reinforced chassis and modifications to the brakes, engine and suspension and the off-road capability of a jeep would carry patrols of two or three officers, who were armed with firearms ranging from MP7 sub-machine guns to Sig handguns and less lethal weapons.

By October 2008, Thomond Park stadium was completed on time and could be viewed from all vantage points across the city. The stadium itself served as an iconic building for a vastly changing city, which had been immensely transformed over the previous decade. In the immediate short-term, things were looking up. Gun-crime in the city had decreased, a fact acknowledged by the gardaí themselves, and senior gang members were in custody awaiting trial. The touring All-Blacks rugby team was coming in November, to officially open the new stadium and, in the build up to the event, the buzz and banter around Limerick was of securing precious match tickets. But when November finally came, the heart was torn out of the proud sporting city in the most cruel and sadistic fashion.

November 8 was a cold and wet Saturday afternoon and captain of Garryowen thirds team, twenty-eight-year-old Shane Geoghegan, played in a keenly contested rugby match against cross-city rivals, Shannon, at Coonagh. Strongly built, Shane was a physically imposing man with a dark beard. Off the rugby field, he was a kind-hearted character. In a hard-fought affair, Garryowen suffered their first loss of the season losing 3-6. It was a result the light blues were not used to, as Shane had led the team to success in the North Munster Gleeson league in the previous season.

He returned home that evening to Clonmore in the Kilteragh housing estate in Dooradoyle. The son of Tom and Mary, Shane grew up on a farm in Clounanna, Patrickswell, County Limerick, before his family moved to Gouldavoher in the city. He was educated in Crescent College Comprehensive and later journeyed across the world, spending time in Australia. On his return home, he became engaged to his girlfriend, Jenna Barry, and worked with Atlanta Aero Engineering in Shannon. Teammates held 'Gagsy' in the highest esteem and within Garryowen football club, the view amongst club members was that he would make a fine President some day. A true clubman, he often lined out twice in the same weekend for separate Garryowen sides and was talented enough to adapt to play in three or four different positions. His family had a fine history with the well-known club, and Shane's uncles, John, Dave and Tony all lined out as forwards for Garryowen.

Life was going well for Shane and exciting times lay ahead for the young man. That evening, he walked the short distance to a friend's house and watched the very first international game to be played in Thomond Park, where Ireland easily defeated Canada. Limerick celebrated the victory and Shane spent the night in the company of his close friends, laughing and joking. He was in a safe place, surrounded by those he trusted.

However, Shane's life was tragically cut short when, later that evening, he was shot just yards from his home.

As news spread across the city on a wintry Sunday morning, Limerick recoiled in horror at the rugby player's death. A Garryowen match against Cork Constitution was cancelled, while those attending a club fundraiser at Limerick racecourse walked out in shock when they heard of the death.

That week while Shane's family and friends prepared for his funeral, council workers put the finishing touches to the city's Christmas lights which New Zealand rugby legend Jonah Lomu was set to illuminate the following week. However, there was little appetite in the rugby-mad city for festive cheer. Limerick has been left completely demoralised.

Mayor John Gilligan summed up the mood: 'We were looking forward to the visit of the All-Blacks next week, but all that seems so inconsequential now.'

Books of condolences were opened in civic offices,

while thousands from around the world visited the *Limerick Leader* website to light virtual candles and leave messages of condolences in memory of Shane. Garda Commissioner Fachtna Murphy was back in Limerick and appealed for public assistance.

Shane's funeral took place at St Joseph's Church in the city, which was packed with over a thousand mourners almost an hour before the service began. More than another thousand waited outside and lined the route to the Mungret cemetery as Limerick came to a standstill. Placed alongside the coffin was a caricature of Shane, a model airplane, the North Munster league cup and a rugby ball. Big, strong men in smart rugby blazers from around the country stood beside frail pensioners wrapped in scarves, silently sobbing. Relatives struggled to make sense of it; men of the cloth reached out in comfort; husbands hugged wives. Everyone, young and old, was incredibly sad, but most were angry and still in shock. They were all united on one point: the violence had to stop.

Bishop Donal Murray made his second passionate plea in 2008 to the city. In a letter to the congregation, Bishop Murray said, 'All human life is precious and murder is never acceptable.'

A harrowing version of the 'Lament of Limerick' was played on violin. The mourners heard the lyrics of 'November Rain' by Guns n' Roses: 'So never mind the darkness, we still can find a way, cause nothin' lasts forever, even cold November rain.' Shane's only brother, Anthony stood up and bravely addressed the silent congregation. With his family, friends and the nation looking on through the media eyes and cameras, he recited a poem by David Harkins called 'Remember Me'.

The entire congregation rose and stood together for a standing ovation in an outpouring of emotion and tears that spread out onto the streets. Shane's coffin was carried out of the church for his final journey; the crowds applauded again, smiled, cried and hugged each other as a clear winter sun shone down on Limerick.

On November 12, the names of twenty-eight-year-old John and twenty-one-year-old Ger Dundon were called out in the local district court, but neither man was present. Ger had been on the run since October 24 when he failed to appear at the Circuit Court for the appeal of his conviction for motoring offences which were affirmed by Judge Carroll Moran. The judge issued a bench warrant for Ger's arrest, following his non-appearance, and he was due in court on November 12 for public-order offences after he was arrested on October 13 at Mill Lane, Henry Street, and charged with offensive behaviour for urinating on a Garda patrol car. He was also charged with being intoxicated to such an extent that he was a danger to himself or others on the same date. John Dundon was also due before Judge Tom O'Donnell when he was charged on October 13 with using threatening and abusive behaviour in Pineview Gardens, Moyross. Bench warrants for the arrests of the two brothers were issued.

That evening, staff and gardaí at Limerick courthouse were shocked when Ger Dundon presented himself to begin his ten-month sentence for the motoring offences. He was locked up in Limerick Prison that night. The following Tuesday, while Munster and All-Blacks rugby players gathered in City Hall for a civic reception, Ger was brought to the adjacent courthouse under armed guard, where he admitted to urinating on the patrol car and pleaded guilty to two charges of offensive behaviour and intoxication. At this stage, Ger had seventy-four previous convictions and received fines totalling €400. Outside, armed detectives and the Regional Support Unit patrolled the perimeter of the building.

When it later became devastatingly clear that there was no ending of hostilities between the gangs, Brendan Kenny explained in the *Limerick Leader* in December 2008 why he met the gangs following a period of calm. The regeneration agencies first met with both members of the McCarthy/Dundons and Keane/Collopy gangs separately before a once-off round the table meeting at their offices in Roxboro in October. Brendan Kenny said it was perfectly understandable that some people would be 'outraged' at the events, but said, 'It is very important to stress that it was only a few meetings, not talks, not negotiations.'

Kenny also admitted to meeting with members of the McCarthy/Dundon gang in Wheatfield prison: 'Maybe it was wrong, maybe we were naive – but the only reason we made such a judgement call was in the interest of the children living in these areas, some of whom have been, or certainly will be dragged into the culture of gangland activity, which will lead to prison and possible early death. If some dialogue could ultimately prevent such behaviour, then it would be worth it. If some dialogue could prevent further awful killings, then it would be worth it.'

In February 2009, an internal split in the McCarthy/Dundon gang occurred after two young men were shot in the Ballinacurra Weston area of the city over the space of ten days. The two men, who were associates of the outfit, were targeted after a falling out over the proceeds of drug dealing. Disturbingly in one of the attacks, a fourteen-year-old, armed with a shotgun, is suspected of carrying out the shooting.

Forty-eight-year-old Christy Keane was released from prison on February 17, having served seven and a half years of his ten-year sentence. A month later, Philip Collopy, one of the two gunmen responsible for the very first murder (Eddie Ryan) committed in the feud, died after he shot himself in the head with a Glock pistol. Collopy was at a house party in St Ita's Street, St Mary' Park, on March 21 and was showing others in attendance how to use the illegal weapon. The ruthless killer took the loaded magazine from the pistol, but forgot about a bullet which was still in the breach. Believing the gun to be empty, Collopy put the weapon to his own head and pulled the trigger. At his removal, the dead man's remains were laid out in military dress with a tricolour draped over his coffin. A Toyota Dyna van with large floral bouquets and one of his horses led the funeral cortege through the city centre en route to the burial.

Before the month of March was out, another ruthless

criminal died. John Creamer, who survived the machine-gun attack when he was shot fifteen times in 2001, was found dead in a flat in London, following a suspected drugs overdose.

Just before this book was completed, another Limerick man lost his life in a shooting incident. Thirty-five-year-old Roy Collins was a popular and loved man. He had two daughters: twelve-year-old Shannon and eight-year-old Charlie. He was engaged to be married to twenty-three-year-old Melissa Crawford that summer, and the couple were putting the finishing touches to a new home in the Ballina/Killaloe area, on the shores of Lough Derg. Roy owned and managed the Coin Castle amusement arcade at the busy Roxboro Shopping Centre. It was located right alongside his father's pub, the Steering Wheel. On April 9, 2009, Roy was at the amusement arcade when he was shot dead.

Another innocent man had lost his life and the city was left reeling again, six months after the death of Shane Geoghegan.

Following the deaths of Shane Geoghegan and Roy Collins, the government brought in tougher legislation in an attempt to crackdown on crime in Limerick. The week after Roy Collins' death, Justice Minister Dermot Ahern announced that surveillance material would be admitted as evidence in criminal trials under the new Criminal Justice Surveillance Bill. The bill enables gardaí, the Defence Forces and officers of the Revenue Commissioners to carry out secret electronic surveillance and if necessary break in to properties to plant bugs to enable them to gather information and intelligence on plans, movements, contacts and methods of operation of individuals and criminal gangs in Limerick. Ahern also announced new measures where crime suspects will face non-jury trials in an extension of anti-terrorism laws. It will also be an offence to be a member of a criminal organisation.

On May 10, in a powerful message against the city's criminal gangs, over 5,000 people, many dressed in red, marched in the city's streets in a united protest against criminal activity. The event was organised by Steve Collins, who was still trying to come to terms with the death of his son. Members of both Shane Geoghegan's and Brian Fitzgerald's families also attended. Many more were too afraid to attend the protest. Defence Minister Willie O'Dea said, 'That is an indication of how far the problem has gone here and how deep the malaise has gripped the city.'

On May 28, a young Limerick man was found guilty of the 2006 murder of Fat Frankie Ryan. The twenty-six-year-old denied the charge in the Central Criminal Court. The sole witness to the incident had identified the killer to gardaí but changed his evidence in court. He refuted the allegations he made in video-taped interviews which were shown to the jury. The witness said they were 'lies' and said 'if I knew who killed him, I wouldn't be alive today'. The jury returned a majority verdict of ten to two. Central to the conviction was the use of legislation introduced by former Justice Minister Michael McDowell in 2006 which allows statements made to gardaí to be used as evidence even if they are subsequently retracted, as they were in this case. This was the defendant's second murder conviction and he had at this stage thirty-nine previous convictions dating back to 1998.

The criminal scene in Limerick is constantly evolving. Wayne Dundon is due to be released from prison in 2010, after completing his sentence for threatening to kill Ryan Lee. When his ten-year sentence was reduced to seven years by the Court of Criminal Appeal in 2008, Wayne Dundon said he intended to return to the UK upon his release. All of Limerick certainly hopes this is the case.

Limerick's problems have clearly manifested themselves in more ways than gang fatalities; innocent people have been killed and childhoods have been corrupted. It is not surprising that methods of addressing such issues were not easily agreed upon. The challenges Limerick faced were like none before in the Irish state, and such uncharted waters required innovative solutions.

15

Towards Regeneration

As head of the agency entrusted with the regeneration of
Limerick in 2006, John Fitzgerald soon realised that the task
set before him was the ultimate challenge:

'I thought about it and a lot of people said to me at the
time, that you'd want to be out of your head in trying to find
a solution for that, because some people took the view that
it was not solvable. I never looked at it that way at all. Being
a Limerick man myself, I was interested in it, that certainly
conditioned my thinking, but probably more than anything
else is the feeling that I could make some contribution to it.
There were different things that could be done, maybe not
that easily, but they could be done.'

A task force was the first solution mooted for Limerick,
but Fitzgerald soon discovered this was the last thing that
was needed:

'Originally the intention was that I would set up a task force that would be modelled on the approach taken in north Clondalkin in the 1990s. I was a member of that task force along with Sean Aylward, who is now the Secretary-General in the Department of Justice. It was quite successful in terms of pulling a lot of different organisations together and it worked quite well and was overtaken by the economic upturn that followed on. The intention was when I came down here; I would identify the various players, pull them together, set up a task force and write a report.

'But I was only here a week and I realised that the last thing Limerick needed was a task force, it was up to its ears with task forces. It is a very small city and I began to realise as you go around meeting different groups, you are meeting the same people across the table, representing different organisations. I decided at that stage that the best thing to do was to draw on my own experience and write a fairly short, sharp and succinct report. The only thing I did was get agreement to involve Brian Cawley from the Institute of Public Administration (IPA). I'd have a lot of tactical and coalface experience, whereas they would have a lot of experience on the more academic approach to it and look at the international experience and what works around the world. So I went to the IPA, got an agreement to involve them and met Brian Cawley and he offered to get involved himself. I was very surprised that he did because he operates at a very senior level, but I was blessed that he did. As well as having the academic background and knowledge, he is a fantastic report writer and a very sharp, shrewd operator and he brought a lot to the experience.'

As Fitzgerald pulled together the full picture for his report to the Cabinet Committee on Social Exclusion, the problems that residents encountered on a daily basis soon became known.

'We met a lot of people, but mainly people from the communities at public meetings in Southill and Moyross. At the time, I didn't really know what I could say to them, I was really there to listen. People genuinely felt very frustrated; there was a lot of cynicism and frustration which was understandable. There were people who were very isolated and alienated from structures and services, which in terms of geography were very proximate to them, but they might as well have been light years away in terms of accessibility.

'The one question that everybody kept asking all the time, any time I met any group or individual was: "Who do we go to and who is in charge?" This is an extraordinary kind of thing in a way because they could see the guards coming around, health and social workers around in the evenings, but it did not work together. There was a huge proliferation of services from 9am to 5pm, Monday to Friday, but the real gap was at night-time and at the weekends, especially when all hell broke loose, when children were out of control, there was nobody available, nobody around and people didn't know where to find them.

'A lot of the problem children were recorded in files and by the time the files had all been processed, the child had moved from a potential delinquent into criminality. So what

I said to them at the time [residents in the deprived estates] was that I was not the police commissioner, I was not the Mayor, I was not the CEO of the Health Service Executive, I am only here as a representative of government ... I promised that I would relay whatever I thought about their situation back to government and I was reporting back to the Committee on Social Exclusion which was chaired at that time by the Taoiseach [Bertie Ahern]. ... I have no bag of money, no rights or politics, but I can promise you that whatever I think needs to be said, will be said. That's what I felt the report had to do. It had to reflect the stark nature of the problem and it was pretty stark.'

In his report in April 2007, Fitzgerald painted a bleak picture of the city's problem areas and their make-up as the Celtic Tiger went into decline. At the time, over 40 per cent of the total housing stock in the city was made up of social housing, with much concentrated in high density areas.

'The construction of large social housing estates in such a confined area undoubtedly helped to create the conditions for problems to develop,' Fitzgerald wrote. He said the reality of life in the estates he visited was 'quite shocking and the quality of life for many people is extremely poor'. Of the four areas, he said, 'Violent crime, related both to gang rivalry and drugs, is now a very serious issue and is gradually extending over wider areas ... Some people who have tried to stand up to the criminals have been intimidated, and there is some evidence that elderly people are being intimidated out of their homes ... The situation in Moyross, Southill, St Mary's Park, and Ballinacurra Weston is extremely serious and must be dealt with as a matter of urgency' to prevent the problems spreading to other parts of the city.

He made several key recommendations. These included an additional 100 gardaí to be deployed to the city and the establishment of a local CAB operation to profile criminals; two State-sponsored regeneration agencies for the northside and southside; improving access and infrastructure; attracting inward investment and the development of the region; a regional task force to be set up to address the city's drug problem and the demolition of 1,000 houses (this figure would later be increased to in excess of 2,000).

With all his experience, Fitzgerald had never before encountered the enormity of the problems that greeted him in Limerick.

'When I went back to the Committee on Social Inclusions, I did make the point that I had spent a lot of my life working in various public areas, but I felt that people were more vulnerable in Limerick than anything or anywhere I had experience beforehand.'

He recalled speaking in 2007 at a sports conference in Punches Hotel the day after he received a letter from Southill residents, expressing their fear that they could not talk openly of the problems in their estates at a public meeting as those making life hell for them were also in attendance.

'I had the letter with me and I read some of it and it struck me that the audience that was there would be the same as you would encounter in the Gresham Hotel. It just struck me that there was this extraordinary juxtaposed position of a sports conference taking place with ordinary people at it and I had a letter in my pocket from a person who lived about half a kilometre up the road in O'Malley Park. I read out a bit of it [the letter] and I said there was this extraordinary situation where we were all there in relative comfort and half a kilometre up the road you had somebody living like this. It was like two parallel universes.

'It showed how vulnerable these residents were, they didn't know where to go. The irony of it is that the availability of resources in the last ten years is much greater than it ever was. Money wasn't the problem, that wasn't the issue, but the situation here in Limerick in my opinion, and I think I know what I am talking about, is worse than it was a decade ago. It had deteriorated fairly dramatically and the vulnerability of people was clear to see. You are talking about good communities and sound, solid people who went about doing their own business and they couldn't do that anymore,' Mr Fitzgerald revealed.

The Galbally man offers a number of explanations as to why the quality of life had deteriorated to such an extent:

'Conditions had got so bad because the conditions that surrounded them were pretty awful. There was a lot of dereliction, burned-out houses, damage and vandalism. Once that gets to a certain point, then the idiots take over and they run the show. There is a tipping point once estates begin to go downhill. I saw it myself. Once the rot sets in and it is not addressed, then they begin to spiral downhill and sometimes it takes no more than two or three people to cause that rot. Things had almost spiralled out of control and I use that word hesitantly.

'I find that in the work I do – especially in local government – when you get in to sort out problems like that, burned-out houses, derelict buildings that are a haven for antisocial behaviour, some people actually want it that way and like to live in the dark. It suits them to live in the dark and they don't want any light to shine upon it. There was an exodus of people out of all these estates who just wanted to get out and there are some awful tales of people who gave up houses and had to get out. It is absolutely intolerable that it should happen.

'What we are really trying to do is restore confidence, where there is none, and it is not that difficult to do that. Once there are people involved with the communities and they see that somebody is in charge, that the system is beginning to reassert itself, they see the State and local government getting involved, then it doesn't take that much to restore confidence. Most of the people are appalled at the way conditions around them deteriorate. These people are the most honest and solid people you could meet anywhere, but even the ones that are involved in antisocial behaviour, some are fathers and mothers and we find that quite a lot of them who are on the edge are getting sucked into this, because it is the thing to do and that is what their role models are doing. We find that when you sit down and talk to them, they really don't want to be in that situation and they certainly don't want their kids to be in it. These are people who have been in trouble all their lives who have two- and three-year-old kids and they really don't want them going down the same track. I suppose you are trying to capture that constituency and win it back. A lot of what Brendan Kenny [Chief Executive of the Regeneration Agencies] has been doing is exactly that, restoring confidence in the communities, trying to create a situation in which the people are prepared to stand up and do the right thing and are encouraged to do that.'

President Mary McAleese returned to visit Limerick in early 2008. On a memorable day, the Irish President met with residents in Southill and Moyross and spoke of her hopes for a 'truly better future'.

In October 2008, after a two-year period of consultations and planning, the cost of the projects became known and the masterplans were finalised. The regeneration of Moyross, St Mary's Park, Southill and Ballinacurra Weston was to encompass a complete transformation of the neighbourhoods. However, for the venture to become a reality, an initial costing of €1.7 billion from the public exchequer was put on the ten-year project. It was also hoped that at least another €1.4 billion would be forthcoming from private investors. When the cost was revealed, the country was in the depths of economic depression, and many scoffed at the projected estimates which they claimed would never materialise.

The Chief Executive of the Regeneration Agencies Brendan Kenny said all involved in the masterplan were very conscious of the new economic environment, 'but we stress that the investment proposed will be required over a ten-year period and that ultimately a successful regeneration project will deliver considerable economic benefits and savings for the State.'

Emphasising the point that the Regeneration Agencies saw the cost as an investment in the future of Limerick's youth rather than a cost, Kenny said the cost of the 'do nothing' scenario in terms of community suffering was not acceptable. He revealed that it costs the State in the region of €90,000 for each prison place and up to €200,000 in high-security prisons, while each student who attained graduate status in education brought an economic benefit of €200,000 to the State.

Just over €647m of public money was earmarked for future investment in Southill and Ballinacurra Weston, along with an estimated €506m of private funds. Proposals include 3,000 new houses to be built in Southill with 800 of these to be replacement homes for current residents and the rest to be sold on the open market. In Ballinacurra Weston, up to 350 are to be provided, with 300 of these allocated to replace existing homes as well as a new purpose-built community centre to serve a variety of sectors. The plans are far-reaching and include the proposed demolition of Our Lady of Lourdes Church in Ballinacurra Weston and Holy Family Church in Southill, which the agency claims 'would allow far more efficient use of the existing churches' footprints. Sheltered and retired housing units were also proposed for both southside areas. The centre of the redevelopment will be at a new Roxboro Cross neighbourhood and a community theatre is also proposed. The existing Roxboro Road Garda station, where officers are already working in confined conditions, is to be extended, and four new parks will be provided where the open countryside joins with Southill. A green sporting corridor will be created along the existing railway lines and will contain a number of playing fields with training grounds, clubhouses and, in some cases, floodlit, all-weather pitches. A proposal was also made for a new college of community, adult and further education on the southside of the city.

In Moyross, it was hoped that just short of €728m would come from taxpayers' money for the mass regeneration, along with €467m of private funds. Almost 2,000 homes are to be built in the northside suburb with a neighbourhood centre for residential, retail, cultural, commercial and medical facilities. The area has always suffered from limited connectivity to Limerick. To address this, a train station located in the heart of the community is planned, along with a dual carriageway linking Moyross to the main Limerick-Ennis Road and further access roads in the suburb, which has previously been served with one road, ending in a cul-de-sac. Additional community facilities, such as a Garda station, a regional park and sports park are in the plans, and the green area of Delmege Estate is proposed as a new business park, to create up to 2,000 jobs, including smaller units for start-up industry. The northside regeneration agency said the plan proposes a new Moyross, 'which will be one of the most vibrant and sustainable towns in the country'. It is hoped that the new public spaces and amenities of Moyross will be key to attracting people to visit, move to the suburb and stay.

If finances allow, it was hoped that St Mary's Park would receive almost €300m of public money, which the northside regeneration agency hoped would be boosted by a further €425m from private investors. The objective of the regeneration agency is to unlock the potential of King's Island as a major resource for the sustainable growth of St Mary's Park. Island Avenue will form the central thoroughfare and two road bridges at the northern end will link the estate to Thomondgate in the west and Corbally in the east. Including residential areas, seven quarters are suggested with Island Place forming the local town square. A wetlands quarter and a new park complete with playing fields, riverside walks, fishing piers and a small marina form a perimeter around a large section of King's Island.

Just over two months after the plans were unveiled, 1,900 assembly workers in Dell were told they were to be made redundant in a devastating blow to the city and wider region. The effect of the country's second biggest employer losing two thirds of their Limerick workforce has delivered a severe blow to supply and service companies.

The prospect for future private investment in the regeneration areas in 2009 seems light years away. However, John Fitzgerald believes it can and will succeed. 'Yes, it is absolutely realistic. We are talking about a ten-year span and it is an investment in the future which will pay for itself over the long term. It is an investment; it is repayable,' he said.

There are three phases of the regeneration of Limerick's estates: social, economic and physical. According to

Fitzgerald, the social regeneration is the most important and challenging 'by a long shot'.

'When something awful happens like the death of Shane Geoghegan or when the two Murray children were burned, when the awfulness of that comes across, it is almost as if the rest of the country suddenly remembers that there are problems here, a deeply embedded problem that hasn't been solved. There is a reaction, an outbreak of "get in the army and open up Spike Island and lock them all up". You could send the entire Irish army into places like this with all the weaponry at their disposal, but it will not solve the problem. It might quieten it down for a few weeks, as long as they are there, but it is not a solution to anything. In fact, if anything it is too heavy-handed and can make the situation worse, because it can alienate more of the community, so it is not exclusively a policing problem.

'There are some people who are beyond redemption and we have to deal with them and in a very tough way, but I think the police here been very, very good. Former Chief Supt Willie Keane and his people have a very good record. They can be very proud of what they have done. At the same time, Willie Keane will be the first to accept what I have always said: that is not a policing solution. The best they can ever do is to hold the line and deal with problems which they have to.'

Fitzgerald was not perturbed by the Irish economic crisis for such a mammoth project.

'Even if the economy hadn't turned on its head, if somebody came along and told me that we had €1.6 billion available in the morning, I wouldn't take it, because I wouldn't know what to do with it. You don't build a house on a foundation of sand; you have to get the get the sand sorted out and put in a proper foundation and then go and build a house on it. So there are social issues that have got to be sorted out before you put a brick on a brick and it will take a bit of time to do that, but it doesn't cost an awful lot of money to do it. An awful lot is using resources that are there in a different and more organised way than they were before. So a lot of what is going on, at the moment, is preparatory work for the longer term regeneration.

'I have seen remedial works in Southill, renovating old houses into new houses at enormous cost, and I have seen it before in Fatima Mansions and places where the social conditions that surround them are left untouched and within two or three years, those remedial schemes are gone. The houses are locked up and closed up again, so you are really just throwing good money after bad unless you get in and address the root causes of the problems.

'You have to deal with the core issues in the knowledge that by the time you get to the end of the process, that a lot of the people, who are serious problem cases, that their influence and numbers involved will have diminished. That is the experience; that the size and scale of the problem diminishes as you go along. While I have people saying to me, "You have to deal with that family there and that family in another place who will pull apart anything that is done", that is not true. I am pretty confident with the changes in the environment. People who have a vested interest in creating hell and mayhem will slowly begin to realise that they have a vested interest in behaving themselves and the numbers who will do the opposite, will be fewer and fewer. You will find that when you get to the end of the line, you are talking about a small number of people and you will have to deal with them almost on an individual basis.'

Fitzgerald believes Limerick can provide a template to help resolve future similar problems in other areas of the country:

'Limerick is unique in a whole lot of ways for reasons that are well documented. You have an intense level of anti-social activity in a very small area. There is a fair intensity of social problems all within a confined area. It is a template, in that if we can deal with the problem here, it would certainly be a fairly clear indication that you can deal with it anywhere.'

The regeneration plans are bold and ambitious; they offer hope for thousands of families who have suffered so much throughout the decades. The Celtic Tiger may be well gone, but to those living in Southill, Ballinacurra Weston, St Mary's Park and Moyross, it never arrived in their neighbourhoods anyway.

'Every town and city in the country has been developed in the last ten years, but if you were to go overhead Limerick in a helicopter, it is extraordinary the amount of undeveloped land and greenfield spaces all around and near to the city centre,' John Fitzgerald said.

'St Mary's Park is a kilometre from the city centre and look at how much unused land is there. There was a joke in

Dublin at one time, that if you went out on St Patrick's morning wearing green, somebody would build on you. It was really true the extent to which under-used land in Dublin, Galway and Cork was hoovered up for development. It didn't happen in Limerick for a whole lot of reasons and the extent of under-utilisation of land around the city centre is remarkable.

'I think Limerick has a unique case for financial incentives, and such incentives have an extraordinary capacity to whet the appetite of private-sector developers who haven't all lost their money. There are a lot of guys out there who have been working very hard for the last ten years who have the resources and are looking for new opportunities.'

Fitzgerald – like many in Limerick – believe that efforts on future development need to be concentrated within the city:

'My view is that the centre of Limerick needs to be consolidated; there is a serious problem here. You have the city centre which is looking good, but is fragile and a whole lot of shopping centres outside the city centre which are thriving. This has led to a necklace of underdeveloped land in between. I think the city needs to consolidate the centre here very fast and build it up and around it, creating jobs with offices and shops and new residential and commercial developments. Why the hell are we going out ten or fifteen miles to build houses and shops? In terms of spatial planning and anything you care to mention, it makes sense to build up and consolidate the city centre and we are trying to convince government that Limerick is unique.

'Limerick is the gateway for the Mid-West and the potential is enormous, but it is pointless talking about it, because it will not be realised until it is quite clear that these problems are being sorted out. We don't have to have everything solved; it won't be sorted for about ten years, but you have to be seen to be making serious progress before investors will take you seriously.' Fitzgerald concluded.

Limerick State solicitor Michael Murray has an intimate knowledge of those who have come before the courts and the problems of his native city.

Murray has worked in the position of Limerick State solicitor since January 1, 1980, and has been in prime position to note the changing face of criminality in Limerick throughout preceding decades. According to Murray, it is too easy to blame the current problems in Limerick on the foundation of the city's deprived estates. Social inequality and a lack of opportunity also held great sway:

'I'm not convinced that all of the problems relate to the way in which all of the estates were set up. There was a lot of thought put into their design. The physical planning isn't as bad as it's made out to be. The architect who designed O'Malley Park did so with the intent that houses were built in clusters with spaces at the back of each house that was supposed to create little pockets of smaller communities. The thinking behind this was good; but social deprivation and the lack of job opportunities at that time militated against the ideas that were in his mind at the time.

'The problem was social deprivation; there just weren't the resources. We were very economically weak at that particular time, and that is going back to a period in the late 60/early 70s, when we were losing traditional industries such as the bacon industries – Mastersons, Shaws and Clover Meats who were all big employers. In addition, you had Ranks. All these big sources of employment were lost and were not replaced quickly enough. Allied to that then, you had generations who had been unemployed, had fallen down into a poverty trap and were housed in these areas. That is where the cancer started.

'I wouldn't necessarily say the physical planning was badly thought out. It was just simply that the social planning wasn't there and it wasn't possible to have any social planning because there were no resources for it. There were no jobs available for the unemployed, and the jobs enjoyed by those fortunate to be employed were eventually lost. The people who had been in employment were getting the first call on replacement/new jobs and this meant that the people who were in long-term employment remained so. As a result, long-term unemployment became a generational thing in a large number of families. Then, obviously when people become demoralised, certain social ills begin to break out and it festered from there.'

The State Solicitor said he is completely behind the regeneration project but has reservations about some of its dealings. Working in the courts, he acknowledges that he comes across people whose parents and grandparents were also brought before the judicial system:

'We are dealing with third and fourth generations of people that started out on this road.

'The disturbing thing is that the Regeneration Board is now dealing with these gangs and talking with them [in 2008]. What lesson are they going to teach them? ... It is very misguided in my view of the regeneration boards, to be dealing with these people, because the only lesson they are going to learn is: if they play ball with certain sections of society, they will learn that they can vest themselves with a veneer of respectability and they can get on with their nefarious deeds behind closed doors. The problem is that once these people begin to learn how to work the system, that is when we are in real trouble and it seems to me that the regeneration board are trying to teach them how to work the system. The place to interview people who are involved in feuding is either in a Garda station or a courtroom.

'There is absolutely no two ways about it. Regeneration, physical and social, is absolutely essential for the city. Anyone who reads John Fitzgerald's report can see that is the central meaning of that. In my view, everybody should support the aims and objectives of regeneration.'

However, he has apprehensions about the State body:

'The make-up of the Regeneration Board is a matter of concern. It does not seem to contain anybody suitably qualified both in the area of urban design and planning or in the socio-economic sciences, who would have the ability to critically assess the proposed plans and manage the implementation of same.

'Further, they have employed certain experts in the area under consultancy contracts. My understanding is that there are different consultants for the northside and the south-side. ... The consultants who are engaged report directly to the regeneration boards. My concern is they don't meet one another – that they are kept apart; there is no synergy, and there is no inter-consultation between consultants. They are not all singing out of the same hymn sheet. I find it difficult to understand why people from different disciplines, look-ing at the same problem in one small area, should be split and kept apart. I would have thought that an exchange of ideas, round-table discussions, brain-storming sessions and the like would bring forth some very interesting and novel ideas. None of this is engaged in and I find that rather extraordinary. I just find that the whole way in which the Regeneration Board is being implemented is quite disturbing.

'But most disturbing of all is the fact that they are talking to the criminals and the whole point of regeneration is that the criminal fraternity would be made irrelevant to the com-munities concerned. Their power, influence and ability to threaten and impose their will would be diminished by regeneration, and the people now living in those areas are looking at the Regeneration Board, what they are doing and the way in which they are interacting and dealing with the feuding gangs.'

Murray also issued an ominous warning if the city's crimi-nal gangs are not taken head-on and tackled in the near future:

'The threat of the gangs to the State as it stands is nowhere near the level of threat that was there from the subversives back in the 60s and 70s. However, unless the problem is tackled it will become a problem of equal proportion, because it is inevitable that somebody is going to dominate the whole criminal scene in Ireland and the gangs in Ireland. When that happens, the person will be strong enough to organise all the various gangs in a way that will be impossible to combat. If we don't win the battle now against the gangs, we could very well find that we have a much worse problem in ten years' time, where not only will the battle be lost, but the war will be lost.'

Witness intimidation is a problem that regularly stops successful prosecutions in Limerick's courts. Murray believes a new solution is needed:

'We have four or five criminal sessions every year. In every criminal session over the last five years, there is at least one if not two cases that fall by the wayside as a result of intimidation of witnesses. That is only the tip of the iceberg, because an awful lot of the cases do not even get to that stage or get off the ground. They won't go to the gardaí because of intimidation.

'People have to be encouraged. It has to be pointed out to them "when good people do nothing, evil men prosper". So we have to appeal to people's sense of civic duty and one has to be encouraged to be brave, because if we don't stand up to these people, then all could be lost.

'Michael McDowell did introduce a system whereby the statements of witnesses could be introduced in evidence. It was basically based on a Canadian system. We have tried to use that legislation, but by and large it has been unsuccessful, because the juries are at all times told the onus is on the prosecution to prove cases. If there is any reasonable doubt, then the person accused must get the benefit of that doubt. The difficulty with introducing the evidence by way of statement, as provided in legislation, is that the person in the witness box is saying, for one reason, or another, they didn't make the statement or are disowning the statement in some other way. On the other hand, the jury is being asked to accept the veracity, or truth, of the statement and inevitably, when they are told they must give the benefit of the doubt to the accused then they find it is nearly always the case that they [the jury] can't accept the evidence of the statement. Having said that, this piece of legislation has had its uses and was instrumental in achieving a conviction for murder in the recent past.

'I have been suggesting for some time we should borrow something from the continental system of Jurisprudence, and that we should appoint a number of circuit judges as investigating magistrates or investigating judges and give them the power to participate in the investigation on behalf of the State. They should have the power to take statements and record them in a court environment by way of audio and video recording. If this is done in the course of the investigation then the jury could be shown these statements if they [witnesses] are not prepared to give evidence and the jury should only see those statements as recorded and make up their own minds.'

Calls for the internment of known criminals on the sworn

affidavit of a Chief Superintendent did not sit well with the State solicitor:

'I haven't been impressed by what I might call off the wall, right-wing comments, made in reaction to Shane Geoghegan's death. The rule of law is very important and it is very important that whatever we do, we respect the human rights of the individual, and the guards have demonstrated time and time again, that they are well able to do that job if they are given the resources. While the law has to be fine-tuned to deal with particular problems, we must respect human rights, and it is very disturbing to hear senior politicians in opposition making suggestions that are off the wall.'

Murray believes that Limerick has been let down by the failure of the government to quickly implement the policing measures as sought by John Fitzgerald in 2007:

'The pre-eminent issue at the moment is that there is an over emphasis on the physical regeneration. But what is much more important is the social regeneration and the policing of the areas. The policing has not been undertaken in the way John Fitzgerald has sought. ... There has been considerable additional resources provided, and there is no doubt that there has been a considerable level of improvement in the policing of the areas, but unless you go the whole hog on this, you are not going to get the long-term results that you need. I also think that political control in the way in which we police our state has not helped. Garda management has been forced by different political forces to devote resources in a way that has resulted in a diminution of resources in the fight against crime.

'In particular, if you take Limerick, I have seen the divisional traffic corps in the last two or three years beefed up considerably and I think there are about forty members of the traffic corps, soon to get a Garda inspectorate to supervise from new offices. It has got a huge amount of resources, both in terms of manpower and equipment over the last three years, but at the same time, the divisional drugs squad has been decimated. The divisional drugs squad has one detective sergeant and three detectives with a number of other personnel assigned to it. Just generally speaking, that is crazy. Road-traffic enforcement has become huge on the political agenda and it is an area that requires attention, but when you see it getting more attention than the drugs scene in Limerick, you begin to wonder, who has lost the plot.

'The other area, I suppose we have to think about is what level of policing do we want or do we need. In my view, the policing per capita now is less than it was back in 1957 and when you take into account the way in which the country has grown, and the huge numbers of specialist units created, that means that the ordinary policing of this country has diminished considerable over the last fifty years. I believe that the absence of ordinary members of the Garda force within the community is a big handicap to policing and, while we are a small enough country, I think we do need more guards. When you talk to those in power, they say we have better police numbers than Britain or France and so on, but I am not so sure these countries are properly policed at all and I don't think we should be comparing ourselves with other jurisdictions. We have our own peculiarities; we have our own problems and we should address them in our own way.'

* * *

What is offered in this book is a view of how Limerick's crime problems have evolved. Not all violent acts, crimes or deaths have been covered in these chapters. Thousands of people across Limerick each have their own story to tell. Some have, but many fear they cannot or are afraid of retribution if they do so. Because of the conditions that fermented and developed in Limerick, primarily in the areas of Moyross, Southill, St Mary's Park and Ballinacurra Weston, many violent incidents have occurred and have had a massive and negative impact on life in the city.

Every generation will encounter some difficulties, and in Ireland violence has featured in some form for every generation. This dark episode in Limerick's story comes down to drugs, control, families and a deep-rooted hunger for vengeance amongst a people, who have chosen their own brand of morality, which is now permeating down through the generations.

The solution to such difficulties is elusive. It is not one which can be answered legally or by law enforcement. Often when these resources are called upon, the problems have gone beyond their remit and the key actors are never to be found centre stage. Gardaí in Limerick are becoming more advanced and sophisticated than at any other time in Ireland. However, community policing will not prevent a father from desensitising his son and teaching him the merits of Kalashnikov use, or repair the mental damage to an eleven-year-old who decides he wants to kill members of the other gang when he is old enough. Mandatory sentences will not change the belief of a brother who feels he must have a gun for his sixteenth birthday. Normal rules don't apply in these microcosms of Irish society, where economic prosperity, and a sense of opportunity and hope for the future have not featured, and where human values have been diminished beyond all recognition.

During the Troubles of the 1970s and 1980s, many people were reluctant to travel to Northern Ireland. The subversive elements once at play in the North have often been compared to Limerick's feuding gangs, and, as a result, Limerick tends to suffer the same stigma.

The portrayal of Limerick in the media is so often at odds with the overall reality of the city – a city passionate about sport, a city with a dynamic and cosmopolitan heart and a pride in its history. As John Fitzgerald said, the problems in Limerick are unique and far beyond anything he had seen before. Despite the phenomenal work done by gardaí in Limerick, it will take more than law enforcement to deal with the city's deep-rooted problems. Getting to the core of the difficulties is the task; and reclaiming a decent standard of life for Limerick's citizens is what is at stake.

These pages have outlined the most peculiar and the

most brutal of the atrocities in Limerick in recent years. In choosing to read this book, knowledge of the web of gang-land activity in Limerick may have been sought. Tracing the allegiances and divisions of Limerick's criminal underworld has been no easy task. In asking how Limerick's feud began, many people expect the answer to lie in the story of one family, and their spiralling quest for vengeance from another. That is not how Limerick's problems began. If it is difficult to trace the emerging factions of criminality in Limerick, then understanding the central issues that triggered the criminality is even more complex. Without proper social supports and systems, people previously not involved in criminality were almost forced to become involved. For many living in the troubled estates, the thin line between law-abiding society and the chaotic criminal world became less of a choice and more of an inevitable decline. Of course there were others who consciously blazed a trail to lawlessness; many of these have come to their reckoning with the rule of law. Legislation introduced specifically to tackle Limerick's problems has sparked academic debate throughout the country, as due-process advocates cross swords with crime-control zealots. The most recent measures were introduced in May 2009 with Justice Minister Dermot Ahern's announcement that gang-related offences will now be tried in the Special Criminal Court unless the DPP consents otherwise. These new measures negate the need for juries and civilian witnesses. It is one more step towards treating gang members as paramilitaries. Whether these measures will work remains to be seen. Dealing with the key criminal figures has exerted and transformed Ireland's justice system. Dealing with the breakdown in social structures in Limerick's estates will be one of the greatest challenges undertaken in the history of this young state.

However, that is what it is proposed to do in Moyross, St Mary's Park, Southill and Ballinacurra Weston, with regeneration, because all Irish citizens have a right to live in a functioning society. There are many variables at play: how the key individuals involved undertake that task; how they consult with one another; how they consult with and take account of the people in these communities; how to rebuild; how to get stakeholders on board; how to sustain it; how to deal with those who persist in criminality; and, by no means least, how it will be paid for as the nation finds itself immersed in a global recession. Regeneration will need the assistance of law enforcement and the courts – a united approach to tackle the combined issues. The hopes are that Limerick will ultimately become a modern city, comparable with the best in Europe. What will be an even greater strength in Limerick's trajectory is that Limerick knows what can happen if it gets it wrong. Given the commitment of the main players in the regeneration, the hopes are that maybe this time Limerick can get it right, and, in doing so, will come of age as a modern, successful, functioning city.